WITHDRAWN

**MY
FAMILY
SHALL
BE
FREE!**
THE
LIFE
OF
PETER
STILL

Peter Still

MY FAMILY SHALL BE FREE!
THE LIFE OF PETER STILL

Dennis Brindell Fradin

HarperCollins*Publishers*

Library of Congress Cataloging-in-Publication Data
Fradin, Dennis B.
  My family shall be free! : the life of Peter Still / by Dennis Brindell Fradin.
    p.   cm.
  Includes bibliographical references (p.).
  ISBN 0-06-029595-3 — ISBN 0-06-029328-4 (lib. bdg.)
    1. Still, Peter, b. 1801—Juvenile literature.   2. Slaves—United States—Biography—
Juvenile literature.   3. Afro-Americans—Biography—Juvenile literature.   4. Still
family—Juvenile literature.   5. Slavery—Kentucky—History—19th century—
Juvenile literature.   6. Slavery—Alabama—History—19th century—Juvenile
literature.   [1. Still, Peter, b. 1801.   2. Slaves.   3. Afro-Americans—Biography.
4. Still family.   5. Slavery—History.]   I. Title.
E444.S848   2001   00-044862
973'.0496073'0092—dc21
[B]

Typography by Robbin Gourley
1   2   3   4   5   6   7   8   9   10
❖
First Edition

For my father, Myron Fradin, with love

CONTENTS

Graphics Credits

For their assistance, the author thanks:

Alabama Department of Archives and History

Hebrew Union College Library, Cincinnati, Ohio

Sandra M. Rayser, Research Associate, the Historical Society of Pennsylvania

Edward Skipworth, Special Collections and University Archives, Rutgers University Library

Alvetta S. Wallace, Gibson County, Indiana Historian

Special thanks to Judith Bloom Fradin for picture research and archival photography

MY FAMILY SHALL BE FREE!
THE LIFE OF PETER STILL

Note from the Author

Between the 1500s and the 1800s, twelve million Africans were shipped to North, South, and Central America as slaves. In the United States two million people—a sixth of the nation's population—were slaves by the year 1830. Less known is the fact that, during the time of slavery, many African Americans lived as free people. By 1830 the United States was home to 320,000 "free blacks," and by 1850 the number had risen to 435,000.

Slaves were liberated in several ways. Five thousand black men helped the United States win independence by fighting in the Revolutionary War (1775–1783). Once the war ended, many black troops were freed as a reward. Thousands of other African Americans escaped southern plantations and fled to the North, where slavery wasn't allowed. Still others were freed by the terms of their owners' wills. In addition, some people bought their freedom. Slaves generally worked from sunup to sundown five days a week and half of Saturday. By doing extra work in their "off-time," slaves might earn pennies and dimes, even quarters. Eventually a person could accumulate the thousand dollars or so needed to purchase his or her liberty.

Achieving freedom was an incredibly soul-stirring experience. Harriet Tubman told a friend that, after she escaped slavery in 1849, the entire world appeared different to her. "I looked at my hands to see if I was the same person," she recalled. "There was such a glory over everything. The sun came like gold through the trees, and over the fields, and I felt like I was in Heaven."

Yet, wonderful though it was, freedom had a sad aspect for former slaves. Generally they had to leave loved ones behind in bondage. Peter Still, the hero of the true story you are about to read, belonged to a family divided by slavery. Left behind with his brother when his parents and sisters were liberated, Peter had to wait half a century for his chance at freedom. But by then he had a wife and children of his own who were also slaves.

All of the dialogue and attitudes attributed to the people in this book are based on firsthand nineteenth-century printed sources, mainly *The Kidnapped and the Ransomed*, written by Kate Pickard with Peter and Vina Still's assistance; *Early Recollections and Life of Dr. James Still* by James Still; *The Underground Railroad* by William Still; the Peter Still papers at Rutgers University in New Brunswick, New Jersey; and the Still collection at the Historical Society of Pennsylvania in Philadelphia. Additional information has been provided by descendants of the Stills, who for 130 years have held a yearly reunion to celebrate their family's long struggle against slavery.

Often runaway slaves were captured.

CHAPTER I

"THE KIDNAPPING"

It was summer when Peter and his brother Levin were "stolen" from the Griffin plantation in eastern Maryland. Peter later calculated that it was probably 1806, and that he was six years old and Levin eight at the time. However, it could have been a year earlier or a year later, and the boys could have been a year younger or a year older. Slaves weren't permitted to read or keep calendars, so they were unable to determine exact dates or even know when their birthdays were.

The two boys were standing by the door of their family's cabin on this particular summer afternoon when a white man drove up in a gig—a two-wheeled carriage pulled by a horse. The stranger stopped the vehicle and walked over to speak to the boys.

"Where is your mother?" asked the stranger, who smiled at them in a friendly manner. All that day—a

Slave being whipped

Sunday—they had worried about the whereabouts of their mother and their little sisters, Mahalah and Kitturah. Peter and Levin had awakened in the morning to find their mother's and sisters' beds empty, and there had been no sign of them since. As best the boys could figure, their mother and sisters had gone to church early that morning but for some reason hadn't yet returned.

"Don't know, sir," answered Levin. "We reckon she's gone to church."

"Well, jump up here with me, and I'll take you to your mother," the stranger offered. "I'm just going to church. What!" he added, looking them over with disapproval. "No clothes but a shirt!" He told them to go inside and put on their trousers. They didn't have any, however, for slaveholders commonly did not provide slave children with pants or dresses until they were about ten years old.

"Well, go in and get blankets then!" ordered the stranger. "It will be night soon, and you will be cold. Come quick!"

Eager to be taken to their mother, the brothers ran inside their cabin and found blankets. Then the stranger placed them in the gig between his feet. He whipped his horse, and off they went.

From their resting place on the floor, Peter and Levin could not see, but they soon realized that they had traveled far beyond the church. When the boys asked where they were going, the stranger reached into his bag and gave them each a little sweet cake, assuring them that they would soon be with their mother.

After traveling for some time, the stranger missed a curve and the gig suddenly overturned in a stream. Fortunately the boys were not hurt. The stranger pulled the children from the water, righted the carriage, and continued on.

At sunset they reached a river. The boys saw a boat landing with many sailboats, rowboats, and rafts, but not a sign of their mother and sisters. Fearing that they were being kidnapped, the brothers burst into tears and continued to cry until the stranger explained that their mother had gone farther off. He took more sweets from his bag and handed them to Peter and Levin. Then he directed them to walk along a plank and down into the hold of a large boat. If they continued on, he promised, they would certainly find their mother.

The boys spent the next several days traveling—sometimes in wagons, mostly in boats—with little to

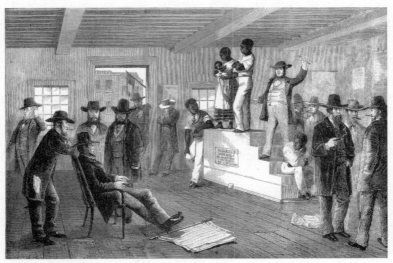

Slaves being sold at auction

eat or drink. When left alone, as often happened, they cried and held each other for comfort. Yet, because of what Peter and Levin knew about their family's past, they still held out hope that they really were going to meet their loved ones.

A while back, when their sisters, Mahalah and Kitturah, had been hardly more than babies, their father, Levin Sr., had done a remarkable thing. He had announced to the family's owner, Saunders Griffin, that he would kill himself rather than continue to live in slavery.

"I will die before I submit to the yoke anymore!" Levin Sr. had told Mr. Griffin.

Instead of whipping him for his insolence, Griffin had made Levin Sr. an offer. If he would "overwork"— meaning do extra chores in his off-time—Griffin would pay him a few pennies per hour. Levin Sr. agreed to the proposal. At the end of a long workday, he remained in the field, plowing by moonlight. When the bell signaling the end of work was rung on Saturday, he continued to weed, chop wood, or run errands around the plantation. After a year or two he was exhausted— but he had saved a few hundred dollars. He turned the money over to his master. True to his word, Saunders Griffin wrote out papers declaring that Levin Sr. was a free man.

A free man! How the family had celebrated in their cabin in the plantation's slave quarters. But Levin Sr. couldn't enjoy freedom while his wife and four children remained slaves. Before saying good-bye to his family, he told his wife, whose name was Cidney, a secret. He was heading up north, to a certain place not far from Philadelphia, Pennsylvania, near the Delaware River. Cidney should wait awhile, then flee with the four children and join him in his new home.

Cidney waited as her husband advised. Then one night, in about 1805, she fled with her four children.

Cidney (Charity) Still

By day they hid in barns and swamps. Following the North Star, they traveled at night through woods and fields. Levin and Peter, who were only about seven and five years old, helped carry their little sisters, and antislavery people drove them part of the way in a wagon. After traveling more than a hundred miles over many nights, they found Levin Sr.'s cabin in a remote woodland.

They had a joyous reunion with their husband and father. For a short while they lived together as free people in a Free State. Levin Sr. found work in a sawmill, and Cidney and the children gathered berries and mushrooms for the family to eat.

Levin Sr. had thought his secret spot would be safe. But Saunders Griffin sent men to capture Cidney and the children. One day when Levin Sr. was away working in the sawmill, slave hunters approached the family's cabin in the woods. They seized Cidney and her four children and drove them in a wagon more than a hundred miles back to the Griffin plantation in Maryland.

Mr. Griffin was so angry at Cidney for running away that he wouldn't allow her to return to the slave quarters with her children. Instead he placed the children under the care of an old slave woman and locked their mother up every night in the attic of his mansion. Week after week Peter's mother had to sleep like a caged animal in the dark garret. Each morning at dawn she was let out to work in the field, only to be locked in the garret again after dark. Finally, after three months, Saunders Griffin proclaimed that Cidney had been "cured of running away" and allowed her to rejoin her children in the slave quarters.

But Peter and his brother and sisters knew that their mother had not been "cured of running away." In fact, she wanted to escape more than ever. On the summer day when their mother and sisters disappeared, Peter and Levin had wondered if the three of them had run off again to find Levin Sr. And now, as the boys sat in the hold of a slow-moving boat, they prayed that the stranger truly was a friend who was taking them to their family.

The brothers did not know how long or how far they traveled. The stranger told them that just one more wagon ride would take them to the place where their mother was living.

Their hopes renewed, the boys climbed into the wagon with the man, whom someone called *Mr. Kincaid*. The wagon rolled along past beautiful horse pastures. Finally they entered a town with stores, blacksmith shops, churches, and large homes. Mr.

Kincaid drove the wagon to a brick house. He said they would find Cidney there.

Mr. Kincaid took the boys inside and spoke for a few minutes to a Mr. John Fisher, a white man who seemed to own the house. Then Mr. Kincaid and Mr. Fisher led the boys into the kitchen.

"There, my boys!" said Mr. Kincaid. "There is your mother—we have found her at last!"

A black woman was in the kitchen, but she was a complete stranger.

"No, no, she's not our mother!" shrieked the brothers. "Please, sir, take us back!" they begged, clinging to Mr. Kincaid. He pushed them away and rushed out the door, never to be seen by Peter or Levin again.

As the boys continued to call for their mother, Mr. Fisher slapped them across their faces. "Hush!" he commanded. "You rascals belong to me now, and I'll have no more of this. Here's Aunt Betty—she's your mammy now!"

But the brothers wouldn't stop crying and screaming that they had been stolen from their home. Mr. Fisher kicked and punched them, all the while swearing that he would kill them if he ever heard them say they had been "stolen" again.

Mr. Fisher then ordered Levin and Peter to bed down on the floor of his and his wife's bedroom. Afraid that Mr. Fisher would hear them crying and give them another thrashing, the brothers sobbed themselves to sleep as quietly as they could.

CHAPTER II

"MR. CLAY, WE'VE BEEN STOLE!"

Peter and Levin believed that Mr. Kincaid had stolen them from their home and sold them to Mr. Fisher, but much of what had occurred was a puzzle to them. Over the next few days, a white boy who worked for Mr. Fisher and lived in the house told them what had happened. They were in Lexington, in Kentucky's Bluegrass region, an area famous for breeding horses. Mr. Kincaid had sold them—Levin for $155 and Peter for $150—to Mr. Fisher, who would put them to work in his brickyard when they were a little older. Until then they were to perform chores around the house and help Aunt Betty in the kitchen.

The brothers had learned a lesson from the beating on their first night at the Fishers. They kept blank expressions and quietly did as they were told in Mr. or Mrs. Fisher's presence. Only when they were alone dusting furniture in the parlor or weeding in the

Henry Clay

garden did they dare whisper about their past life.

Their biggest question was: What had become of the rest of their family? The brothers believed that their mother and sisters had run off to join Levin Sr., somewhere around the Delaware River near Philadelphia, Pennsylvania. But where was Philadelphia and how could they get there? And why had their mother left them behind? The boys' conclusions were partially correct. What had actually happened was this. . . .

Cidney had decided to make another run for freedom but had realized that taking all four of her children would be too difficult. She decided to flee with her daughters and then find a way to rescue the boys once she reached her husband. Cidney couldn't tell her sons about the plan for fear that Mr. Griffin would whip the information out of them once he discovered she was missing.

Late Saturday night or early Sunday morning, Cidney quietly awoke her two daughters. She tiptoed to the little straw mats where her sons were sleeping, knelt down, and kissed the boys good-bye. Then she, Kitturah, and Mahalah crept out of the cabin. Guided by the North Star, Cidney led her daughters toward freedom.

The journey was so exhausting that, along the way, Kitturah had to be left by the side of the road. Cidney continued on with Mahalah until they reached her husband's cabin, which was on the New Jersey side of the Delaware River. Levin Sr. backtracked, found his youngest child by the wayside, and carried her home in his arms.

Slaves caught escaping were sometimes branded so that they could be identified if they fled again.

As soon as possible Cidney, Levin Sr., and their daughters moved to a place called Indian Mills, situated about twenty-five miles east of Philadelphia, Pennsylvania, in a part of New Jersey called the Pine Barrens. There they changed their names. Cidney became *Charity* and Kitturah became known as *Kitty*. Mahalah and Levin Sr. also may have adopted new first names. Slaves had no last names of their own, but were generally called by their owners' surnames. Formerly Griffin, the family chose their own last name: *Still*, perhaps because Peter and Levin Jr. were still slaves. The four Stills living as free people in New Jersey hid their identities so well that Saunders Griffin never located them.

But Griffin was determined not to have the boys snatched from him. Just hours after realizing that

Cidney had escaped with her daughters, he sold Levin Jr. and Peter to Mr. Kincaid for more than a hundred dollars apiece. Kincaid took them more than five hundred miles from Maryland to Lexington, Kentucky, where he sold them to Mr. John Fisher at a handsome profit.

Peter and Levin Fisher, as they were now called, desperately wanted to escape to search for their family. But never having been taught to read or understand a map, they had no idea how to begin. If they asked Mr. Fisher about it, they knew, he would beat them mercilessly. They had to find someone who sympathized with them and would take them to their parents.

Slave escaping

In addition to their town home on Main Street, the Fishers had a plantation just outside Lexington. Peter was sometimes sent there to tend the cows or deliver messages. A prominent politician named Henry Clay lived across the road from this plantation. In 1806—about the time that Peter and Levin arrived in Lexington—Clay was elected to the United States Senate.

Peter was often allowed to go across the road to play with the Clays' sons, Theodore and Thomas, after he finished his tasks at the plantation. One day Peter confided to Theodore that he and Levin had been stolen from their mother. Theodore said that Peter should tell his father, who would do something to help.

"Oh, Levin!" Peter whispered, the next chance he had to be alone with his brother. "I reckon we're going back to Mother. Master Theodore Clay says his father'll send us back if we tell him how we got stole!"

Soon after, Peter was running an errand in Lexington when he saw Mr. Clay standing near the county courthouse. He ran up to the senator and eagerly said, "Oh, Mr. Clay! My brother and I, we've been stole!"

"Who stole you, and where were you stolen from?" Mr. Clay asked.

"From our father and mother who live near the Delaware River around Philadelphia. Won't you please send us back to our mother, sir?"

"To whom do you belong?" asked Mr. Clay.

"Master John Fisher, on Main Street, but we want to go back to our mother, sir."

"Well, my boy," said Senator Clay, "you carry this

letter to Major Pope and I'll attend to the matter." Peter took the letter the senator had been holding and ran off, thinking that he and Levin would soon be restored to their parents. But Peter never heard another word from Senator Clay on the subject. If Clay checked into the matter, he learned that Mr. Fisher had proper title to the boys.

After their first year in Lexington, Levin was sent to work in the brickyard. Early each morning he trudged off to the brick factory and returned each night dirty, exhausted, and sometimes with whip cuts across his back. Peter still thought about running away, but the brothers spoke less about finding their family, for Levin barely had the energy to eat his supper of corn cakes and bacon before falling asleep.

At the age of nine, Peter was sent to the brickyard, too. Now he understood why his brother was always tired. Like Levin, Peter was assigned to be an "off-bearer." He piled finished bricks into a wheelbarrow, wheeled them to the warehouse, stacked them, then returned for the next load. The ovens and kilns heated up the factory until the place seemed like hell. But if Peter, Levin, or any of the other slaves stopped to rest or wipe away the sweat—*wham!*—down came the foreman's whip.

When Peter was about thirteen and Levin fifteen, they heard distressing news. Mr. Fisher was selling his brickyard and the fifteen slaves who worked it. At least the brothers had been together at Mr. Fisher's. Now they faced the prospect of being sold apart, never to see each other again. Fortunately Mr. Fisher sold them both to another Lexington brickmaker, Nat Gist, who paid $450 apiece for them. The brothers remained together, but the change of owners brought new hardships.

Gist, a nearly sixty-year-old former Revolutionary War soldier, owned a large brickyard worked by about twenty slaves. He drove his slaves very hard and provided them with little food and clothing. Moreover, he was a heavy drinker and, when drunk, he was especially cruel.

Soon after purchasing Levin and Peter, Mr. Gist came home drunk. He ordered Peter to scatter a bundle of oats on the ground for his horse, which the boy did. But when Gist looked in the yard, he became enraged, and asked Peter why he'd thrown the oats about.

Suddenly Mr. Gist struck Peter on the head with his cane, and ordered him to the house. Once there, Gist told Peter to take off his shirt and cross his hands.

Gist tied Peter's hands together and whipped him until blood poured from his back and the boy begged for mercy.

Although he treated them harshly, Nat Gist must have thought Peter and Levin would be useful around the house because he made them stay with him instead of out in the slave cabins. The brothers had to serve the old man supper and wait on him after working all day in the brickyard. Whenever he came home drunk, they had to carry him inside and put him to bed. Gist never praised the boys, but he flogged them often to "teach them lessons."

Peter and Levin had been at Nat Gist's for a time when a "Negro Sabbath school" opened in Lexington.

Despite laws throughout the South forbidding the education of slaves, there were a few Sunday schools that taught slaves to read the Bible. The authorities looked the other way as long as the slaves' owners didn't object.

Peter figured that learning to read and write would help him and Levin escape. Then he could write to someone in Philadelphia who might help find their parents. But Nat Gist made it plain how he felt about the school. He announced that he didn't want Sunday school teachers meddling with *his* property, and if he heard of one of his boys going near the school, he'd give him such a flogging that he'd never need any more education.

Peter decided to take a chance anyway. One Sunday morning he ran through the woods to the Sabbath school. When the teacher asked Peter for his pass, he answered that he didn't have one.

The teacher said he wasn't permitted to instruct slaves without the consent of their masters.

Peter knew that telling a lie about his master could get him whipped, but he couldn't miss this opportunity to learn to read and write. He said that his master didn't care about him coming and would give him a pass next Sunday. The teacher allowed him to remain and study the alphabet with the other slave children.

The following Sunday Peter again appeared at the school and once more made up a lie. Again the teacher permitted him to stay for the lesson.

Peter was so excited about learning to write his name that he came to the school on the third Sunday with another lie prepared. His master had left on a trip early that morning, before he had the chance to ask him for a pass, Peter said. Growing suspicious, the teacher let him stay but warned that the next Sunday Peter must have a pass.

On the fourth Sunday Peter again came to the school door with the hope that he could bluff his way in. "Pass?" asked the teacher.

"Ain't got none," Peter boldly replied. "Master Nattie says, don't need none."

This time the teacher refused to admit him. Peter walked home, deeply disappointed. In his three Sundays of school, he had learned the alphabet, and he could spell his name and read and write a few words. But he didn't know enough to write a letter.

There didn't seem to be any way that he and Levin could inform their parents of their whereabouts.

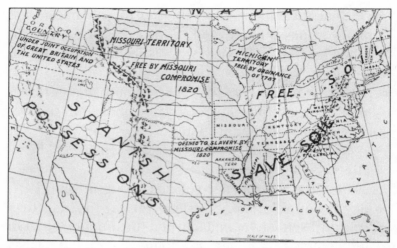

Map showing free and slave soil in the United States in 1820; Kentucky was slave soil.

The Pine Barrens of New Jersey

CHAPTER III

"WE SAW HARD TIMES"

If they could have escaped from Nat Gist, Peter and Levin would have had to travel six hundred miles northeast through five states—Kentucky, West Virginia (then part of Virginia), Maryland, Delaware, and New Jersey—to reach their family.

At first Levin Sr., Charity, Mahalah, and Kitty Still lived in constant fear that Saunders Griffin would track them down. They had chosen an excellent hiding place, however. A region of sand, swamps, and scraggly pine trees, the Pine Barrens were inhabited largely by people who wanted to get away from everyone else.

Not much is known about the Still family's life in the Pine Barrens. We do know that Levin Sr. and Charity Still had more children—*many* more. Counting Mahalah and Kitty and their two sons left in slavery, the couple had a total of eighteen children, the last of whom was born in 1821. Eight of them died young, including their first child, Ann, who was born while Levin Sr. and Charity were slaves.

The Stills' son James later described growing up in his huge family. "I well remember our house," he wrote in his book, *Early Recollections and Life of Dr. James Still.* "It was an old log house, one story high and an attic, with one door, a large fireplace, and no glass windows. I think there were two rooms on the first floor and one on the second. People were poor in those days, and had no stoves to heat their houses, nor carpets on the floor."

Accustomed to hard labor, Levin Sr. maintained several jobs to support his family. He worked in a sawmill, chopped and sold wood, and made charcoal. There was a school in the area that was open to both white and black students, but the Still children could attend it only during the winter and on rainy days. At other times they had to work. The children grew vegetables in their family's garden, gathered berries, fished, chopped wood, and worked around the house.

"In those days we saw hard times—frequently short of food and clothing," James Still later recalled. "I remember one time we were out of bread and meat, and almost everything like food, and father left home in the afternoon to go in the country and get something for his family. He stayed all night, and returned the next morning with flour and meat on his shoulder. Mother made a cake and fried some meat."

Another time the family was eating the first meat they had seen in weeks when their old black cat, Jacko, grabbed James's portion out of his hand and began chewing it. James was so hungry that he caught Jacko, pulled the meat out of the cat's mouth, and ate it himself.

Charity and Levin Sr. were demanding parents. "My father was very strict with his children," James wrote. "We were not allowed to run about to play on Sundays like the other children. All of us that could read must stay about home and read the Scriptures, and those that could not read must study their spelling-lesson." Like other former slaves, Levin Sr. and Charity were accustomed to physical punishment. When his children misbehaved, Levin Sr. whipped them, quoting from chapter 13, verse 24 of the Old Testament's Book of Proverbs: "He that spareth his rod hateth his son: but he that loveth him chasteneth him betimes." Or, as people more commonly said: "Spare the rod, and spoil the child."

Although Levin Sr. and Charity didn't often talk about their years in slavery, they discussed one aspect of their former life with their sons and daughters. They told them about the family's "two lost children," Levin Jr. and Peter. Mahalah and Kitty had dim memories of their older brothers, which faded with time, and of course the younger children didn't know them at all. Levin Sr. and Charity Still learned that their two oldest sons had been sold by Saunders Griffin and taken somewhere farther south. But they didn't know the identity of the boys' new owner or exactly where they had been taken.

They could only hope that by some miracle, their lost sons would be restored to them one day.

CHAPTER IV

"LEVIN, I SHAN'T SEE YOU NO MORE!"

Nat Gist operated his brickyard only during warm
weather. Over the winter he closed his brick
factory and rented out his twenty slaves to
various people in Lexington. Their first three winters
with Gist, Peter and Levin were rented out as house
slaves. They cleaned, ran errands, cooked, and served
meals to the white people who hired them.
Occasionally Peter and Levin saw Mr. Gist collect the
rent money on his slaves. That gave the brothers an
idea.

Some slaves were allowed to "hire their own time."
This meant that their owners let them make their own
work arrangements—for example, cleaning houses or
working as a barber or nurse. They were obligated
to pay their owners a certain amount per year—say
$150 or $200—but could keep whatever they earned
above that. A few slaves who hired their own time
saved enough money to purchase their freedom, much

Workers in a southern tobacco factory of the 1800s

as Levin Sr. had done.

Peter and Levin talked about hiring their own time and buying themselves out of slavery. Usually, though, slaves weren't permitted to do this until their middle years, by which time they were thought to be too old to run away. Talking to other slaves, Peter and Levin also discovered that buying one's freedom often didn't go as smoothly as it had in their father's case. They heard many stories about slaves who were cheated out of their freedom, like this one about a stable hand they knew.

Spencer was known around Lexington for healing sick and injured horses. His owner, Mr. Williams, allowed him to hire his own time, and he was in such demand as a horse doctor that he managed to save money. One day Spencer asked what it would cost to buy his freedom. Mr. Williams set the price at $1,000. Over the next few years, Spencer gradually paid his master the money. He had paid $975 and was just $25 shy of the amount required to free himself when Mr. Williams suddenly denied promising him his liberty and sold him.

Spencer's new owner had heard what happened and said it was shameful. He, too, promised to free Spencer for $1,000. To keep from being cheated again, Spencer asked for a receipt each time he paid his owner. When Spencer had paid all but $70, however, his master sold him and left town.

His third master said Spencer's receipts were useless, but assured him that, for $1,000, he would grant Spencer his freedom. After several more years Spencer paid off every last cent. He was given papers, which, although he couldn't read, he believed were his freedom papers. The papers were actually a bill of sale. Spencer had been sold again, not granted his liberty. The unfortunate man was locked in chains and led with other slaves to the cotton fields of the Deep South.

Despite such horror stories, the brothers decided that, if the chance ever arose, they would try to hire their own time and buy their freedom. Nat Gist would never let them purchase their liberty, they were certain, but perhaps one day they would have an owner who would.

Slaves being led away in chains

Peter and Levin had been with Nat Gist for four years when there was troubling news in the Gist household. Nat Gist was unmarried, but he was fond of his brother's three sons. These nephews had decided to leave Kentucky to farm and open a store in Alabama. Gist announced that he planned to retire and send six of his slaves to assist his nephews. None of his slaves wanted to go, for it meant leaving friends and relatives and moving into the Deep South, which had a reputation for having especially harsh and unhealthy conditions for slaves.

Early that fall Nat Gist made his choice. Levin was among the six slaves he would present to his nephews, but Peter wasn't.

The prospect of being separated was agony to the brothers. In all their suffering, Peter and Levin had always had each other. "Oh, Levin!" Peter cried. "If they take you way off there, I shan't never see you no more, sure!"

Sobbing as he held his younger brother in his arms, Levin said, "Oh, yes, Master Nattie says he gonna bring all his slaves to Alabama next year when he comes there."

Peter didn't believe it. "Master Nattie's too old to go to a new country," he cried. "Oh, Levin, there ain't no use living in this here world. I shan't see you no more!"

A few weeks later preparations were completed. On a lovely October morning in 1817, Nat Gist's nephews rode off on horseback with their six slaves. Through his tears, Peter watched his brother disappear in the distance.

Soon after, Nat Gist closed his brickyard. During the year that he remained Nat Gist's property, Peter was rented to a Lexington family as a house slave and also worked on the plantation of Gist's brother a few miles outside Lexington. All that year Peter's thoughts turned continually to his brother. Had Levin survived the journey to Alabama? Had he died of the fevers that claimed many lives in the Deep South? Peter heard nothing about his brother until the summer of 1818 when one of the nephews, Andrew Gist, returned to Kentucky for a visit. He reported that everyone who had moved to Alabama was well and that the Gist lands there were rich and beautiful.

Not long after, Nat Gist's health failed. Everyone believed he had worn himself out by years of drinking. Nat Gist died on September 13, 1818. Peter tried to look sad as they buried the man who had been his owner for five years, but inwardly he rejoiced. By the terms of Nat Gist's will, his remaining slaves were to go to his nephews down in Alabama.

In a short while Peter expected to be with his brother.

CHAPTER V

"Been Getting Married, Hey?"

On December 20, 1818, Peter departed Lexington with John Gist, one of his dead master's nephews. Riding out of Lexington on that cold Sunday morning five days before Christmas, Peter thought about bolting and heading north. He was about eighteen years old, five feet eight in height, one hundred fifty pounds, thin but muscular and strong, and he knew that he could overpower John Gist and ride away. But he also realized that his chances of reaching one of the nearest Free States, Ohio or Indiana, were slim. The woods were filled with "slave patrols"—bounty hunters who searched for runaway slaves. Besides, Peter couldn't bear the idea of never seeing his brother again.

Within two or three days, their route took them past Hodgenville, Kentucky. Nine years earlier a boy who would become president of the United States had been

Slaves picking cotton

born near Hodgenville. But in 1816 seven-year-old Abraham Lincoln and his family had moved north to Indiana, because his father wanted to raise his children in a state that didn't allow slavery.

On Christmas morning Peter and his young owner arrived at Hopkinsville, Kentucky, where John Gist's aunt lived. Ten years earlier Jefferson Davis had been born near Hopkinsville. Davis would one day become Abraham Lincoln's great adversary. He would lead the Confederate States during the Civil War. However, the war that would tear the nation in two was more than forty years in the future that Christmas morning. Peter and John Gist remained in Hopkinsville until January 3, 1819, and then resumed their journey.

A short ride from Hopkinsville brought them to the Tennessee border. A day later they reached Nashville, a growing town that would later become the capital of the state of Tennessee. They rode quickly, fording numerous streams, and soon crossed into Alabama. At eleven o'clock on the morning of January 6, they arrived in Bainbridge, a settlement along the Tennessee River near the towns of Florence and Tuscumbia in north-western Alabama. They had completed the three-hundred-mile journey in eight traveling days, averaging nearly forty miles per day on horseback.

Peter's heart pounded when they arrived at the Gist plantation, which consisted of just a few log buildings. He was told that Levin was off working somewhere in the fields. A few minutes later a wagon drove up, with Levin and some other slaves on it. Even before the wheels stopped rolling, Levin jumped down from the wagon to greet Peter. The brothers hugged each other and wouldn't let go. Tears of joy rolled down their cheeks.

Nat Gist's three nephews—John, Andrew, and Levi Gist—ran the plantation in Bainbridge, a newly established village consisting of about thirty white families and their slaves. Although they worked for all three brothers, Peter and Levin were legally the property of the oldest, Levi.

The Gist brothers were enterprising young men. They had planted cotton, which was becoming so important to the South that people called it "King Cotton." They had also built a general store on their property, in which they sold dry goods, groceries, and liquor, and they operated the Bainbridge Post Office.

Peter was immediately sent to work with Levin in the fields. From dawn to dusk they planted, weeded, and picked cotton. The work was difficult, but they were young and strong and happy to be together again.

Not that they were reconciled to remaining slaves forever.

At night in the cabin they shared in the slave quarters, the brothers whispered about escaping. They knew that they were even farther from their family near Philadelphia than they'd been in Kentucky, although by how much they couldn't say. Yet, somehow, Peter and Levin assured each other, they would one day have a chance at freedom.

In the meantime they found it comforting to talk about their family at the end of each day. They often discussed the last time they had seen their mother and sisters and recalled how nearly fifteen years earlier they had been taken away by Mr. Kincaid. They tried to imagine what life might be like for their loved ones, living as free people. One thing the brothers often argued about was the spot on one side of their mother's face. Peter claimed it was a mole, while Levin insisted it had only been a blemish.

Peter and Levin worked on the Gist brothers' plantation for about three years. Then in late 1821 Levi Gist married Thirmuthis Waters, a young woman from Nashville, Tennessee. Levi bought a larger plantation seven miles outside Bainbridge and moved there with his new wife and slaves.

Levi Gist wasn't the only member of his household who had fallen in love. The Gists had a neighbor named Jimmy Hogun, whose slaves included a young woman named Fanny. Levin and Fanny met, and began to spend their Sundays together walking through the woods and talking. Peter grew jealous as his brother seemed more interested in being with Fanny than with him. On a spring day in about 1822 Levin approached Levi Gist about marrying Fanny.

Peter and Levin had considered Levi Gist the best master they had ever had. He didn't often whip his slaves and fed and clothed them decently. But when he heard Levin's marriage plans, he exploded in anger. "What put the idea into your stupid head to go to Jimmy Hogun's to hunt for a wife?" he said. "No, you can't have Fanny. You may have a wife and welcome, but no boy of mine shall marry a girl of Jimmy Hogun's!"

"But, master," protested Levin, "I don't want nary another wife, sir."

"Don't talk any more about it!" commanded Gist. "Hunt up another girl that will suit you better."

Levin walked away, crestfallen. He knew what the problem was. Slave children automatically belonged to the mother's owner. If Levin married Fanny, their children would belong to Jimmy Hogun. Levi Gist couldn't stand the idea of losing thousands of dollars worth of potential new slaves to Hogun.

Still, on Sundays Levin continued to walk a few miles to Jimmy Hogun's to visit Fanny. Then one Sunday he married her without his owner's permission. Slaves weren't allowed to have wedding or funeral ceremonies with ministers, so Fanny and Levin simply pledged their love for each other in front of Peter and a few friends. After that they were considered married.

When he heard about it, Levi Gist was enraged. He forbade Levin to visit Fanny, but Levin defied him, continuing to walk to the Hogun plantation Saturday night or early Sunday morning to spend a day with his wife. Gist caught Levin returning from one such visit and ordered Levin whipped. But just as the overseer raised his arm to begin, Gist stopped him. Let this be a warning, he said. If Levin visited Fanny again, he would receive a whipping he'd never forget.

Levin didn't heed the warning. One Monday morning at dawn, when he returned from Fanny's cabin at the Hogun plantation, Levi Gist was waiting for him. Gist had Levin stripped and tied up, and this time he took the whip and began striking Levin himself. Had Peter been present at this monstrous beating of his brother, he undoubtedly would have attempted to stop it. A witness reported that the more Gist whipped Levin, the angrier he became, until he seemed like a madman. Gist whipped Levin until strips of bloody flesh hung from the slave's back. Finally, after 317 strokes, he suddenly threw down the whip.

Levin was carried to his and Peter's cabin. For many days Peter nursed his brother's terrible injuries. He rubbed bacon fat on Levin's wounds and gave him small amounts of food and water from a gourd. Over a period of weeks, Levin recovered somewhat.

One night Levi Gist entered Peter and Levin's cabin. "I have acted hastily, while in a passion, and I am very sorry," he said, and then left.

Never again did Gist try to stop Levin from visiting Fanny on Sundays. But Levin's health was never the same following his severe beating. Just twenty-five years old, he now walked with difficulty and could no longer do field work. Levi and Thirmuthis Gist took Levin into their mansion to do housework. Peter was also brought in to work in the "big house" as a cook, housekeeper, and waiter.

The brothers rarely talked about escape anymore, for it hurt to think about something that seemed impossible. If Levin found it difficult to walk a few miles to his wife's cabin, how could he travel hundreds of miles north to the Free States? No, Peter thought, all they could do was make the best of the situation and enjoy what they could of life. Although the flame of hope did not die out completely, it burned low in Peter's heart and would remain only an ember for many years.

A house slave

A mile from the Gists' residence was the plantation of Bernard McKiernan, whose wife was Thirmuthis Gist's sister. One of Peter's new duties was to drive Mrs. Gist in her carriage on her frequent visits to Mrs. McKiernan and sometimes deliver notes back and forth between the sisters.

At first Peter disliked going to the McKiernans, who were said to be especially cruel to their slaves. Then one day a young house slave of the McKiernans' caught Peter's eye. She was shy and sad-looking, yet Peter noticed that she brightened up whenever he approached. He always tried to say a few kind words to her while he waited for Mrs. Gist to finish chatting with her sister.

Soon Peter realized that he looked forward to

seeing the slave girl, too. He began to visit her on Sundays and ask her to accompany him on walks. Her name was Lavinia, but everyone called her Vina. She was just fifteen years old—ten years younger than Peter. Vina had lived with her mother and brothers on an Alabama plantation, but her owner had fallen deeply into debt and had sold Vina away from her family. She had been purchased by a doctor in Courtland, Alabama, who owed money to Bernard McKiernan. Short of cash, the doctor gave Vina to Mr. McKiernan in trade.

Not long after they began spending their free time together, Peter and Vina decided they wanted to marry. This pleased the McKiernans. They had taken a fancy to Peter and hoped that, if he married Vina, the Gists might be willing to sell him to them.

Because of what had happened to his brother for marrying a girl "off the plantation," Peter was reluctant to ask the Gists if he could marry Vina. He decided to wait for a time when the Gists were especially pleased with him to ask permission.

In May of 1825 the Gists announced that they were going to visit Lexington, Kentucky. They had planned the trip for more than a year and had told Peter that he could drive them there. Everyone knew that Peter had been looking forward to seeing old friends in Lexington, but now, suddenly, he did not wish to go.

Levi Gist was surprised. He thought there was nothing Peter would like better but told him he could remain at home and that Uncle Frank could make the trip instead. He was referring to a slave rather than to a relative, for it was customary among southern whites to call older black people "aunt" or "uncle."

Levi and Thirmuthis Gist entrusted their slaves to the care of relatives and departed for Lexington with Uncle Frank driving their carriage. Peter had made a decision. Rather than risk asking for permission, he would marry Vina while the Gists were gone. Peter hoped that they wouldn't punish him when they returned and found out what he had done. Vina agreed to the plan, as did Mr. McKiernan, who thought it would be a good trick on his brother- and sister-in-law.

The couple were married on Saturday night, June 25, 1825, in the slave quarters of the McKiernan plantation. Levin, Fanny, and a few friends witnessed the wedding. Cato Hodge, an old slave who had heard and memorized parts of the Bible, said a few words and pronounced them husband and wife. The bride wore a cast-off white dress that Mrs. McKiernan had thrown away.

When he returned from Lexington a few days later, Levi Gist was displeased to learn what Peter had done, but he did not react as he had to Levin's marriage. "Well, Peter," he said, "you've stolen a march on us since we've been gone—been getting married, hey?"

"Yes, sir," said Peter, relieved that his master didn't seem very angry, "I've been getting married."

Master Gist evidently wanted to make up to Peter for what he had done to Levin for the same offense. Rather than punish the newlyweds, the Gists and the McKiernans engaged in a kind of tug-of-war over Peter and Vina. The Gists asked the McKiernans to sell them Vina, while the McKiernans tried to convince the Gists to sell them Peter. But no one would budge, and

Inside a slave cabin

Peter and Vina continued to live apart.

At Christmastime the McKiernans and their slaves moved into a house in Bainbridge. Every Saturday night, when his work week was over, Peter walked about seven miles to be with his wife. Vina lived in a cabin with other slaves at the McKiernans' new home until Peter decided to build a cabin that she could have to herself all week and share with him on Saturday night and Sunday.

Peter chopped down trees and hauled the logs to the McKiernans' slave quarters. He worked at building the cabin all day Sunday, week after week. Sometimes, when the moon was high, he continued building all through Sunday night, departing early Monday morning to be back at work in the Gist house by dawn. In April of 1826 he completed the cabin, and Vina had her own place to live.

About the time that Peter married Vina, Levi Gist purchased a slave who was a skilled shoemaker. Gist allowed this man to teach Peter his craft. On weeknights, after completing his tasks in the Gist house, Peter made shoes for other slaves and occasionally for white people. He was paid for his work in pennies, dimes, and quarter dollars. Peter used the money to purchase household items for Vina in Bainbridge. He bought her clothing, a few dishes, a cupboard, and a flour barrel. One Saturday night he proudly carried a clothes chest to his wife. Peter wanted Vina to be as comfortable as possible in the summer of 1826 because she was expecting their first child.

On September 12, 1826, in the little slave cabin Peter had built, a baby was born to Vina. Peter couldn't see the child right away because it was a Tuesday and he wasn't allowed to leave the Gists'. Four nights later he hurried to his wife's cabin and saw his new son for the first time. He and Vina named the boy Peter Jr. Peter had enough money from his shoemaking to buy some cloth for Vina to make new baby clothes for their son.

Peter was following the course he had decided upon after Levin's vicious beating. He was enjoying life as best he could. And when he was with his wife and child, Peter was a happy man.

William Still

CHAPTER VI

"WILLIAM, I WOULD RATHER DIE THAN LIVE A SLAVE"

Five years before the birth of Peter Jr. in an Alabama slave cabin, another member of the family was born in a log house in the New Jersey Pine Barrens. William Still entered the world on October 7, 1821. He was Charity and Levin Still's eighteenth and final child. William's family included three older sisters—Mahalah, Kitturah, and Mary—and four older brothers—Samuel, James, Charles, and John. Seven other brothers and sisters born in New Jersey died young.

William grew up knowing that he had two other brothers who were slaves somewhere in the South. In a letter written to a friend as an adult, William recalled that he had often heard the story about his parents leaving two sons behind in slavery:

> *I must tell you what I never mentioned to you before, that my parents were once slaves. They lived in the State of Maryland, but feeling a strong desire for liberty, my father (as I have*

often heard him say) resolved that he would rather die than live a slave. He was allowed the privilege of purchasing himself, and by the earnings of his own hands he soon paid the sum demanded, and obtained his "free papers."

My parents had four children, and the desire of freedom rested so heavily upon the mind of my mother, she [escaped to] the State of New Jersey. But before Mother had long enjoyed what she prized so highly—liberty— she and all four of her children were pursued, captured, and carried back to Maryland. For a while she was confined nights in a garret, to prevent her from making a second effort for freedom. But it was all to no purpose. She made a second flight, taking her two youngest, which were girls, and leaving her two boys, Levin and Peter.

I shall never forget hearing my mother speak of the memorable night when she last fled. She went to the bed where her two boys, Levin and Peter, were sleeping—kissed them— consigned them into the hands of God and took her departure again for a land of liberty. My mother's efforts proved successful, though at the heartrending consideration of leaving two of her boys to the disposal of slaveholders. Those unfortunate boys were sold soon after my mother's escape. All that she ever heard of them afterwards, was that they had been sold far South.

William had many responsibilities during his childhood. By then his family had established a farm. William grew vegetables and apples and sold them to neighbors, and he tended the pigs and chickens. He also helped his father cut wood and make charcoal.

Like his older siblings, William went to school only during bad weather. Most of his friends and neighbors were white, so he was shocked by the bigotry displayed by some white classmates. Once, as he was returning home from school, a crowd of white boys pushed William over the side of a bridge into about four feet of water. Even some of the teachers seemed to be prejudiced against their black students. During class one day, perhaps because William didn't know the answer to a question, the teacher made him stand outside the school wearing a dunce cap. William's father, Levin Sr., happened to visit the school that day and saw his youngest child being humiliated. Enraged, Levin Sr. stood up for his son and told off the teacher in front of the other students. Levin Sr. withdrew William from the school and didn't send him back until there was a new teacher three years later.

But his education didn't suffer. As the baby of the family, William had many teachers. His brother Samuel, fourteen years older than he, was good at arithmetic and taught William to work with numbers. His sister Mary, thirteen years his senior, wanted to become a teacher and practiced by teaching William to read and write. James, nine years older than William, hoped to become a doctor. James "treated" William, pretending to give him "shots" with pieces of pine bark. James also taught William the names and medicinal qualities of the trees and wildflowers in the woods.

What little recreation William had seems to have consisted of swimming and fishing in the old mill pond near his home. He was a serious boy, and very diligent and dependable. If his mother told him to pick apples, he filled bushel baskets with the fruit. If his father told him to chop a cord of firewood, he went to work with his ax and piled up the wood neatly. Intelligent and thoughtful, he was generally quiet and listened well, but when called upon, he was a fine speaker. William also loved books and often spent his evenings by the fireside reading as he shelled corn or peeled apples. He subscribed to the *Colored American*—one of the country's first antislavery newspapers owned and published by blacks—and from reading it he learned more about slavery and race relations.

William found it astonishing that people could keep other people in bondage just because of the color of their skin. It seemed even more incredible that he had two brothers he might never see because they were being held as slaves. He looked at the map of the United States, with "Mason's and Dixon's line" separating the northern Free States from the southern slave states, and wondered where in the South his brothers were living.

William grew up at a time when slavery was a fiercely debated issue in the United States. Many people called *abolitionists* wanted the federal government to

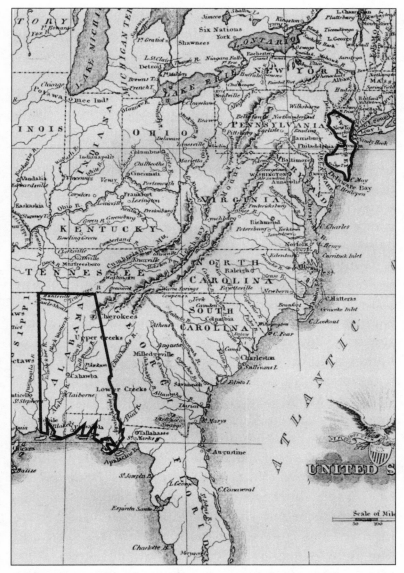

While Peter and Levin were slaves in Alabama, their brother William was growing up eight hundred miles away in New Jersey near Philadelphia, Pennsylvania.

outlaw slavery everywhere. The abolitionists issued newspapers and made angry speeches about the cruelty and injustice of human bondage. Slave owners spoke with equal passion about "States' Rights"—meaning that they thought each state was entitled to decide for itself about slavery. Around the time of William's birth, Kentucky statesman Henry Clay had helped work out a deal between the supporters and opponents of slavery. Called the *Missouri Compromise*, it allowed slavery in the new state of Missouri but outlawed it in the new state of Maine. However, many Americans were convinced that it was just a matter of time before the nation went to war over slavery.

Young William lived near a hotbed of abolitionism. Philadelphia had the most free black people of any U.S. city and was home to the Pennsylvania Anti-Slavery Society. Philadelphians didn't just *talk* against slavery. Many of them hid escaped slaves in their homes until they could be sent to safety farther north or even all the way to Canada where slavery had been outlawed. Because slave hunters complained that fugitives seemed to disappear—as if in a subway—in Philadelphia and other abolitionist strongholds, the network of hiding places for escaped slaves became known as the *Underground Railroad* or *UGRR* for short. People who led fugitives northward were called UGRR *conductors*, houses where fugitives hid from slave hunters were *stations*, and the homeowners who took in escaped slaves were nicknamed *stationmasters*. People who paid the expenses of transporting UGRR "passengers" were known as *stockholders*.

William Still served as an UGRR conductor at least once in his youth. A neighboring white family named Wilkins were among the Stills' best friends. The Wilkinses were Quakers—a faith that strongly opposed slavery—and they sometimes sheltered runaway slaves passing through the Pine Barrens en route to Philadelphia, New York, or Boston. One day slave catchers tracked a fugitive to the home of an elderly member of the family, Thomas Wilkins. As the slave hunters tried to drag the escapee away, Wilkins and his two aged sisters scooped up shovelfuls of burning coals from the fireplace. They threw the hot coals at the slave hunters, sending them fleeing. The runaway slave was taken to William Still, who led him twenty miles to an UGRR station at Egg Harbor, not far from New Jersey's Atlantic coast.

By the age of twenty, William Still had decided that he wanted to live in Philadelphia to join the fight to end slavery. However, his father, now about sixty-five years old, was ill, and his mother needed him. He couldn't abandon his parents.

On Christmas Eve of 1842, approximately forty years after telling Saunders Griffin that he would kill himself rather than continue living as a slave, Levin Sr. died. He passed away a free man, in his own bed in his own home, surrounded by his loving family. William remained on the farm for more than a year after his father's death to help care for his mother. Then Samuel, the oldest son (not counting Levin and Peter), took over the farm as well as the care of their mother. Now William was free to pursue his dream of fighting slavery.

In early 1844 twenty-two-year-old William Still set out for Philadelphia. He arrived in the city with just three dollars in his pocket but with his head filled with great hopes for the future.

CHAPTER VII

"I'LL CUT YOUR TWO EARS OFF!"

The year following Peter Jr.'s birth was the happiest period Peter Sr. had known since he and his brother had been kidnapped twenty years earlier. During the week Peter and Levin worked for the Gists, doing housework in their mansion and driving Mr. and Mrs. Gist about in their carriage. The brothers counted the days until Saturday night. Then they would eagerly set out—Levin hobbling along the road to visit Fanny, and Peter hurrying to spend the weekend with Vina and their son.

The McKiernans allowed Vina to grow her own cash crops in a little garden patch during her off-time. On many Sundays Vina and Peter tended their corn and watermelons, as little Peter lay in a basket in the shade. Peter sold the crops and the shoes that he made in Bainbridge and used the money to buy furniture and clothing for his family.

Peter didn't realize that Vina was being sexually harassed by two white men during the week, when he wasn't around. One was her owner, Bernard McKiernan. The other was Mr. McKiernan's overseer (supervisor of the slaves' work), Bill Simms.

Although not openly acknowledged, it was common for slave owners to force slave women to have sex with them. Today this would be a crime called rape, but it wasn't so in slave days. Slaveholders owned their slaves' bodies, and legally they could do whatever they wanted to them. It was also profitable for a master to make his slave women pregnant, for the children became his property, too. Many white masters grew rich by selling their own sons and daughters born to slave mothers.

White overseers often considered it their right to rape slave women, too. Their job was to work people as hard as possible and to enforce the plantations' rules, so overseers tended to be brutal men. When an overseer raped a slave woman, the owner usually looked the other way, if he knew about it at all. Besides, a slave child fathered by an overseer was another valuable addition to the plantation.

Mr. McKiernan and Overseer Simms were both in a position to rape Vina if they chose. Rather than force himself on her, McKiernan promised to give Vina presents for Peter Jr. and herself if she would submit to him. Simms took the opposite approach. Vina had been taken out of the "big house" and put to work in the cotton fields under Simms's direct control. The overseer criticized her for not picking enough cotton, and he passed out less food to her than he did to the other slaves. He vowed to continue this harsh treatment unless she had sex with him.

Vina was in a very difficult and dangerous situation. She didn't want anything to do with McKiernan or Simms. Their advances were repellent, but if she angered them, one of them might kill her. She didn't dare tell her husband. Peter would probably attack McKiernan or Simms, and a slave who attacked a white man could be put to death or have his right arm chopped off.

Vina managed to fend off McKiernan and Simms by protesting that she was a married woman. That worked for a while. But one day when Peter Jr. was about a year old, Overseer Simms threatened that, if she didn't do what he wanted, he would whip her nearly to death.

"You might kill me, but I won't never do it," Vina answered.

Simms was true to his word. Shortly afterward he pretended to find fault with Vina's work in the cotton field. He tied her hands with his handkerchief and struck her in the head with the butt end of his bullwhip, knocking her to the ground. Simms hit Vina several more times on her back and head, leaving deep gashes on her bleeding scalp. Then he warned the badly wounded young woman that he'd shoot her if she told anyone why he had beaten her.

On Sunday, when he visited his family, Peter asked Vina about her injuries. "Bill Simms done beat me," she confessed, and then explained why. "But don't you tell nobody," Vina insisted, "for if he finds out I told, he'll kill me, sure."

Peter felt murder in his heart, but he could only walk around his cabin shaking his fists in helpless rage. If he confronted Simms, the overseer might

kill his wife during the week while he was away.
There was no use telling Mr. McKiernan, for Vina's
owner often said that if anybody came to him com-
plaining about the overseer, he'd give them worse
himself.

After the beating Vina began to have terrible
headaches. Suddenly she lapsed into semiconscious-
ness. She spoke incoherently and didn't recognize
anyone, not even her child. The McKiernans sent for a
doctor, who concluded that she had received some
hard blows to the head. He gave her medicine, but
it didn't help. Believing that Vina wouldn't recover,
Mrs. McKiernan sent for Peter, even though it was the
middle of the week. Vina didn't recognize Peter, either.
With his seventeen-year-old wife seemingly near
death, Peter tearfully told Mr. McKiernan about the
beating Vina had suffered at the hands of the overseer.

"Why the devil didn't she tell me?" McKiernan
demanded.

"Because," Peter said in a low voice filled with
anger, "she knowed your rule, that you don't care how
hard an overseer beats your slaves, if they come to you,
they'll get worse."

A few days later Vina began to recover. When she
was able to talk, Mr. McKiernan questioned her in
front of Simms. Vina described what had happened.
The overseer didn't deny anything.

McKiernan cursed Simms for nearly killing a
valuable slave. He also deducted the doctor's bill
plus a certain amount for each day's work Vina had
missed from the overseer's pay and then sent him
packing. Simms rode away and never returned.

McKiernan wasn't just angry at Simms for injuring his property. He was jealous because he still wanted Vina for himself. It took many months for Vina to regain her health. One rainy day, when she was spinning yarn, Mr. McKiernan suddenly entered her cabin and demanded that she have sex with him.

"You got a wife of your own!" Vina answered, heading for the door.

Mr. McKiernan sprang after her, ripping her dress, but Vina fought back fiercely, pulling his hair and scratching his face. The surprised slave owner tripped and fell to the floor.

"I'm gonna whip you well for fighting me!" McKiernan said, rising to his feet.

"If you do," Vina countered, "I'll tell your missus why!"

"You tell her one word," he threatened, "about this here, and I'll cut your two ears off close to your head!" But McKiernan hurried out the door and gave up the idea of raping Vina—at least for the time being.

In June of 1829, when Peter Jr. was nearly three, Vina gave birth to another son. The couple named him Levin, in honor of Peter's brother and father. When a third son was born to them in the autumn of 1831, Vina and Peter named him William, not knowing that the baby had a ten-year-old uncle with that same name. Their daughter Catharine entered the world in 1837 or 1838. Peter and Vina also had four other children who all died by the age of three. Because of the work they would miss, slaves generally weren't permitted to have daytime funerals. Peter and Vina must have buried

Slave funerals were usually held at night.

their babies on a hillside at night by the light of pine torches.

Peter's owners took their three children to Lexington, Kentucky, to visit relatives in the spring of 1830. When the carriage returned, Thirmuthis Gist and her children, dressed in black, were inside, but Levi Gist was not. The night before the Gists were to head back home from Lexington, Levi had died suddenly of a heart attack or stroke. He had been buried in Kentucky.

In the nineteenth century, widows were often forced to sell their husband's property and move in with relatives. For a few days Peter and Levin worried that Mrs. Gist would sell them—perhaps to faraway places where they would be separated from their loved ones. They were relieved to learn that Thirmuthis Gist would remain on the plantation with her children. Her brother-in-law, John Gist, with whom Peter had ridden to Alabama twelve years earlier, would help her manage the property. The slaves were not to be sold, and Peter and Levin would continue doing housework and driving the family carriage.

But in the months following Levi Gist's death, Peter had new cause for alarm. His brother's health had steadily deteriorated since Levi Gist had lashed him so brutally for marrying Fanny nine years earlier. Although Peter saw that Levin was unwell, he didn't realize just how ill he was.

It was customary for slaves to be granted a few days off at the end of the year to spend the Christmas holidays with their families. At Christmastime of 1831 the brothers went their separate ways—Peter toward Vina's cabin and Levin toward Fanny's. As they said good-bye, the brothers expected to be back together shortly after New Year's Day when Mrs. McKiernan wanted them to return to work.

After Christmas Levin took a sudden turn for the worse. On December 28 he began struggling for air. He begged his wife to send for Peter.

"Peter's in Bainbridge," Fanny said gently, knowing that she couldn't fetch Levin's brother in time.

A few moments later, with his last strength, Levin cried: "Peter! Peter! Oh, Peter!" He gasped faintly and moments later he was dead, at the age of about thirty-three.

Early the next morning Peter received a message to hurry to Fanny's cabin. After he arrived and saw what had happened, Peter went outside and cut some wood. He built a rude coffin for his brother and buried him in a slave's nameless grave, with no stone to mark the spot. When Peter finished covering his brother, he burst into tears, remembering all they had shared since Mr. Kincaid had carried them away twenty-five years earlier.

Never in his life had Peter's spirits been so low— nor had the chance for freedom seemed so remote.

CHAPTER VIII

"What's the Use in Living?"

In 1833 Thirmuthis Gist remarried. Her new husband was John Hogun, a relative of Jimmy Hogun, the man who owned Levin's widow, Fanny. John Hogun had a reputation as a rough master whose slaves were driven hard and forbidden to marry off the plantation.

Hogun put Peter to work in the cotton fields, where he labored for the next six years. Peter became a foreman, which meant that he helped the overseer supervise the other slaves. Before dawn he rang the bell summoning the slaves to work. All day he led a work gang, or group of slaves. Before going to sleep at night, he had to make sure the tools were put away and the other slaves were in their cabins.

Working in the cotton fields of Alabama, Peter knew the hopelessness that most slaves felt. He was more than thirty years old, and freedom still seemed to be no more than a dream. What's the use in living? Peter often asked himself. The answer was Vina and their children. His weekend visits with them were all that made life worthwhile.

But he could not protect his children from the cruelties of slavery. By the age of six or seven, Peter and Vina's children were already out in the fields, pulling weeds and scaring birds away from Mr. McKiernan's crops. One day when Peter Jr. was eight or nine, he developed a terrible toothache. He left the field without permission and went to his cabin to tie a rag around his jaw.

The overseer, a man named Burton, followed the child to his cabin and gave him a tongue-lashing for leaving the field. Burton told the boy to come with him to have the tooth knocked out, but Peter Jr. refused.

It was hog-killing time, and Peter Jr. was expected to be out in the yard before sunrise the next morning to help with the slaughter. His aching tooth kept him up late, however, and the boy overslept. Mr. McKiernan, having come to watch the hog killing, asked why Peter Jr. was late.

"Master Peter is laid up with the toothache," said Burton. "I told him yesterday that, if he would come to my house, I would give him something to ease it, but he refused."

Vina, standing nearby, overheard the conversation and spoke up for her child. "My son said he wasn't gonna come to your house 'cause he didn't want his teeth knocked out like he was a horse."

"Was I talking to you?" asked Burton, scowling at Vina.

"No, sir, but you're tryin' to get Peter whipped, just for nothing!"

"Hush your mouth!" ordered Mr. McKiernan.

"I told the truth, sir," she repeated, hoping they would punish her rather than her son.

Just then Peter Jr. appeared, holding his sore jaw. "What's that impudence you were giving to Mr. Burton last night?" demanded Mr. McKiernan.

Peter Jr. politely explained that he didn't want his tooth knocked out.

"Well," Mr. McKiernan told Burton, "you can tie him up to that apple tree and give him the devil!"

Burton tied Peter Jr. to the tree. He struck him with the whip one hundred times and then ordered the crying and bleeding boy to go to work.

Peter learned about this punishment when he came for his Sunday visit. Again all he could do was pound his fists in fury and frustration. The law allowed owners to beat their slaves, while slaves had no legal recourse.

In 1839 Peter heard a rumor that John and Thirmuthis Hogun were thinking about selling the plantation. This was very bad news to Peter. It meant that, once again, he might be sold away from his family. Fortunately, though, John Hogun decided it would be more profitable to retain the slaves and hire them out.

Starting in 1840 Peter was rented to various people who paid the Hoguns for his work. The first year a family named Threat leased Peter to work in their cotton fields. In 1841 Mr. McKiernan rented Peter. Despite the opportunity to be with Vina and his children every day, Peter felt uneasy working for McKiernan. He had begun to hope that one day Mr.

Peter and his family lived in constant fear that they would be sold apart, as befell this family in an 1860s illustration.

Hogun would let him hire his own time and he might save enough money to buy his family's freedom. If McKiernan purchased him, he would be unlikely to allow Peter to hire his own time.

Peter worked alongside Vina in the cotton fields, knowing that he must do well enough to satisfy Mr. McKiernan but not so well that McKiernan would renew his efforts to buy him. Peter succeeded. At year's end McKiernan declared that he had no further need for him. In early 1842 Peter was hired out to James Stoddard, who ran a boys' school in Tuscumbia, a town near Bainbridge.

Peter served as janitor in Mr. Stoddard's school and did chores in his home. Mr. Stoddard was the first master who treated him like a fellow human being, but Peter was now twelve long miles from his wife and children and could visit them only once every two weeks.

At the end of the year, Mr. Stoddard gave up teaching and no longer needed Peter. A minister, Reverend Stedman, then hired him for 1843. Peter maintained Reverend Stedman's church in Tuscumbia—cleaning it, ringing the bell, and building the fire to warm it in the winter. At night Peter waited on Reverend Stedman and his wife, a woman from New England who sometimes talked to Peter about life in the North, where everyone was free.

Slaves who were hired out were expected to visit their owners just before Christmas to see what was planned for them for the new year. But Mrs. Stedman had some extra tasks for Peter, so Christmas of 1843 approached and passed without his going home to inquire about John Hogun's intentions for him. When Peter came home late, Hogun was very annoyed with him.

The Stedmans wanted to keep Peter in 1844, but, out of spite, Mr. Hogun refused. Instead he hired Peter out to John Pollock, a Tuscumbia merchant.

Peter began working for Mr. Pollock on New Year's Day of 1844. He swept out his store, arranged merchandise, and made deliveries with a horse and cart. Now past forty years old, "Uncle Peter" had earned a reputation around Tuscumbia for being trustworthy and dependable. White people who saw him making deliveries around town began asking Uncle Peter to run errands for them, shine their boots, or sweep out their fireplaces. They gave him dimes and half dimes (five-cent coins that the United States issued from the 1790s to 1873) as tips. By the summer of 1844, he had saved fifteen dollars.

Eighteen forty-four was a presidential election year. That August the Whig Party, a political organization that no longer exists, held a convention in Nashville, Tennessee. A number of gentlemen from the Tuscumbia region wanted Peter to accompany them to the convention as a cook. Peter's owners, the Hoguns, gave their permission, and on August 15 Peter and several other slaves set out with about sixty white men equipped with tents, food, and drink.

The group headed north on horseback and in wagons. In three days they reached Nashville, where they attended a rally on behalf of the Whig presidential candidate, Henry Clay. The Alabama men often amused themselves by drinking and singing in their tents during their week in Nashville. Late one evening, when the conventioneers were not paying attention, Peter left the camp and walked down to the river. He understood some of Nashville's geography from overhearing white people's conversations. He knew that this river was the Cumberland and that it wound up through Kentucky, emptying into the Ohio River at the Illinois border. If he could hide on one of the boats steaming past him along the river, he might travel all the way to the Free State of Illinois.

Peter watched the boats churn by, but he didn't see how he could board any of them. Besides, while he yearned for freedom, he couldn't leave without telling Vina and his children that he would come back for them. Peter walked back to the camp and was not even asked where he had been.

After the convention the Alabama men headed back south. They returned home praising the fine job that faithful Uncle Peter had done, never suspecting that he had flirted with escape. Henry Clay, whom Peter had once asked for help as a child in Lexington, lost the election to the Democratic candidate, James K. Polk—one of five times that Clay campaigned unsuccessfully for president.

In 1845, when he was about forty-five years old, Peter was hired out to Michael Brady, another Tuscumbia merchant. Mr. Brady employed him about his store, providing opportunities for Peter to meet many people who tipped him for doing odd jobs.

Through a complex division of property, in 1846 Peter became the slave of John Henry Hogun, son of John Hogun. His new owner hired Peter out for that year to Allen Pollock, a bookstore owner in Tuscumbia. Peter cleaned Mr. Pollock's store and delivered books, which, ironically, he could not read. The job was not very demanding, so for the first time in his life, Peter had several hours a day free. Seeing this, Mr. Pollock made him an unusual—and illegal—offer.

Allen Pollock proposed that, after completing his daily chores around the bookstore, Peter could hire his own time. All Pollock wanted for granting this privilege was $85 a year, the fee the bookseller had to pay John Henry Hogun to rent Peter. Anything Peter earned over $85 during the year, he could keep for himself. Peter promised to keep this arrangement secret, for slaves were supposed to obtain their owners' permission to hire their own time. If anyone asked, Peter was to say that John Henry Hogun allowed him to arrange his own work schedule.

Over the next year Peter worked at numerous jobs around Tuscumbia. If a family's cook was ill, Peter replaced her for a few days. He set tables and cleaned up after parties at the Franklin House, the town's main hotel. He worked as a waiter at Pope's Hotel in exchange for a room in which to sleep. He served as janitor at a girls' school. He painted fences, dug graves, and blacked boots. Each week he paid Mr. Pollock $1.63, which added up to $85 over the course of the year. Vina sewed her husband a leather purse to hold his money. Periodically Mr. Pollock allowed Peter to change his half dimes and dimes for larger denominations, such as silver dollars and half eagles (five-dollar gold pieces). At the end of the year, Peter had saved $75 of his own. With this money added to his previous savings, he had about $100 in his leather pouch by Christmas of 1846.

Peter knew enough math to figure that, at the rate he was saving, he could have $500 in about five years. He was in his mid-forties—well past the age when slaves were considered in their prime—so he believed he was worth only about $500. If he could save $100 a year, in four more years he might purchase his freedom and then find a way to free his family.

Money wasn't the only problem, though. Most white Alabamians were so strongly opposed to freeing slaves that in 1834 the state had enacted a law about it. A person wanting to emancipate a slave was supposed to announce his intentions in a newspaper and then apply to a local court for permission. Moreover, anyone who freed a slave risked being called an abolitionist and run out of the state. John Henry Hogun would never do all that for him, Peter was certain. He needed to find someone who disliked slavery enough to buy him, sell him to himself, then help him to freedom without adhering to the letter of the Alabama law.

Searching for such a person was risky. If John Henry Hogun found out what Peter was attempting, he would punish him as an example to other slaves who hoped to buy themselves. Peter's greatest fear would probably come true: He would be sold far away from his wife and children.

As 1846 came to a close, Peter tried to think of a white person who might go along with his plan. He considered Mr. Allen Pollock, the bookseller who had allowed him to hire his own time. But Mr. Pollock seemed to have done it mainly because that way he got Peter's services for free, not because he was opposed to slavery. Peter didn't think he would help liberate a slave.

He thought of Mrs. Kate Pickard, a teacher at the Tuscumbia Female Seminary. Peter had been hired to clean the school for its opening in early 1847. Mrs. Pickard came from the North and did not hide the fact that she disliked slavery. But, given her views, if she purchased Peter, everyone would know it was with the intention of freeing him.

There was one other possibility. During his first year of hiring his own time, Peter had occasionally worked at a general store in Tuscumbia owned by Joseph and Isaac Friedman. The Friedman brothers had shown him much kindness, and Peter could tell from their comments that they opposed slavery. Something else drew Peter to them. Although they charged fair prices for their groceries, cloth, and various goods, other white people treated the Friedmans like outcasts and called them stingy behind their backs. The Friedmans were the first Jewish people in Tuscumbia and were abused simply because of their religion. They were among the gentlest people Peter had ever known. Such men would surely sympathize with the plight of a slave.

Toward the end of 1846, Peter spoke to the Friedman brothers and asked if they would rent him for the next year should John Henry Hogun be willing. They said they would, so a few days before Christmas, Peter visited Mr. Hogun and told him that Joseph Friedman was interested in hiring him for the next year.

John Henry Hogun called on Joseph Friedman and learned that it was true. The Friedman brothers said that they wanted Peter for 1847. They may have also agreed to pay more than Mr. Pollock offered. Hogun signed the paper to hire Peter out to the Friedman brothers.

Peter went to work for Joseph Friedman and his younger brother, Isaac, on New Year's Day. When Peter wasn't working at their store, the Friedmans let him hire his own time, just as Mr. Pollock had done. Peter continued to sleep at the hotel where he waited tables and to do odd jobs around town. The savings in his leather purse steadily grew. The Friedmans were also very generous, sending clothing and other items home with him as presents for his family.

All that year Peter watched and listened to the Friedman brothers, trying to decide if he dare suggest his plan to them. Everything he observed strengthened his feeling that they sympathized with the oppressed and would help him.

Around Christmastime of 1847 it was arranged that Peter would continue to work in the brothers' store the following year. Peter made a bold New Year's resolution. He decided that he would ask the Friedmans to buy him.

Philadelphia around the time that William Still moved there

CHAPTER IX

"Sad and Thrilling Stories"

In the spring of 1844, William Still moved to Philadelphia, which, with a population of one hundred thousand people, was second only to New York among the nation's cities. The young man was amazed by what he saw. Houses, doctors' and lawyers' offices, hotels, and churches lined the streets. The city's factories produced a large proportion of the nation's steel, locomotives, carriages, fire engines, lamps, glass, and cotton goods. Along the Delaware River, shipbuilding flourished, especially steamship production. Compared to where William had grown up, in the sparsely populated New Jersey Pine Barrens, the city was very fast paced. Horse-drawn carriages sped by so quickly that just crossing the street was a challenge.

Fortunately he knew at least two Philadelphians. His older sisters Kitty and Mary had preceded him to the big city and were doing well. Mary, who had realized her ambition to become a teacher, was now planning to open a private school for the city's black children. William's sisters fed him and provided him with a place to stay until he found a place of his own—a dilapidated wooden shanty on Fifth Street.

Philadelphia was 162 years old when William Still moved there. The city had been founded in 1682 by William Penn, for whose family Pennsylvania was named. Penn called the city *Philadelphia*—meaning "brotherly love" in Greek—because he hoped everyone would live there in peace and friendship.

Benjamin Franklin, its most famous citizen, had helped the city live up to its name, founding one of America's first successful lending libraries in Philadelphia in 1731 and its first general hospital there twenty years later. The nation's first abolitionist organization, the Pennsylvania Abolition Society, had been founded in the city in 1775, with Benjamin Franklin serving as one of its early presidents. Lucretia Mott had helped found the American Anti-Slavery Society in Philadelphia in 1833, and the Pennsylvania Anti-Slavery Society had been founded in the City of Brotherly Love in 1837.

By the middle of the nineteenth century there were twenty thousand black Philadelphians, including some very influential people in the antislavery movement. James Forten Sr. had died two years before William Still's arrival. A wealthy maker of ships' sails, Forten had organized twenty-five hundred black men to defend Philadelphia from the British during the War of 1812. Forten was also an outspoken abolitionist whose daughters, Sarah, Harriet, and Margaretta Forten, carried on his civil rights work. Other prominent black Philadelphians included Robert Purvis, a leader of the

Pennsylvania Anti-Slavery Society (and husband of Harriet Forten), and Stephen Smith, a wealthy coal and lumber dealer.

Robert Purvis

Despite the cooperation among the city's white and black abolitionists, in many ways Philadelphia was as racially divided as the rest of the United States. Blacks generally lived in segregated neighborhoods, sometimes in makeshift huts. Black children attended segregated schools—if they were educated at all. Blacks usually worked at the lowest paying and least desirable jobs: as grave diggers, cooks, washerwomen, domestic servants, barbers, and coachmen.

There was occasional racial violence, especially as European immigrants moved to the city and competed with African Americans for jobs. In August of 1834 a fight broke out between whites and blacks at the "Flying Horses," an early merry-go-round in Philadelphia. The white mob wrecked the ride and then spilled into nearby streets, looking for blacks to attack. At least one black man was beaten to death, and several black churches were damaged or destroyed. Four years later abolitionists opened Pennsylvania Hall, a meeting place where antislavery advocates from around the country gathered, in Philadelphia. Bigots resented seeing white and black people entering the building together, and on the night of May 17, 1838, a mob burned Pennsylvania Hall to the ground. That same year a new state constitution took away the right of black men to vote in Pennsylvania. Black men could not vote again in public elections in Pennsylvania until the ratification of the Fifteenth Amendment to the United States Constitution thirty-two years later in 1870. (American women of every complexion generally could not vote until the adoption of the Nineteenth Amendment in 1920.)

William was disappointed to find prejudice so rampant in Philadelphia, but he had practical matters to consider. He needed a job. Ironically, the first job he found was working in a brickyard, as his brothers Peter and Levin Jr. had done down in Lexington, Kentucky. Dissatisfied with that, he began hauling wood and doing other odd jobs. Such work didn't pay well, so he opened a restaurant in a cellar, where he sold oysters, oyster soup, and a highly seasoned stew called *pepper pot*.

The oyster restaurant attracted few customers, so William closed it and turned the cellar into a secondhand clothing store. That business lasted just a week. Combing the newspaper advertisements, he found a job as a waiter at a hotel for the very low salary of $5 a month. He was thinking about moving back in with one of his sisters—or giving up city life entirely and returning to New Jersey—when he found a job cleaning house and tending the garden for a wealthy white widow, Mrs. E. Langdon Elwyn.

Mrs. Elwyn told William about her experiences traveling in the United States and Europe and encouraged him to borrow books from her large library. She also paid him $14 a month—a generous salary considering she also provided him with a room in which to live. When she moved to New York after a year and a half, William found a similar job working for a retired merchant for another year.

Meanwhile William was learning a great deal about the Underground Railroad. Although Pennsylvania and other northern states didn't allow slavery, a federal law dating from 1793 allowed owners to pursue runaway slaves and return them to the South. Philadelphia was so near the Mason-Dixon line that escaped slaves who fled there were at great risk of being tracked down by their owners. Philadelphia's Underground Railroad workers hid the fugitives, sometimes in secret rooms in their homes. Then the runaway slaves were often sent farther north to Boston, New York, or Canada.

During his first years in the city, William met many Philadelphia abolitionists. He was introduced to Lucretia Mott, who among other things had helped organize the Anti-Slavery Convention of American Women in 1837. He became close friends with Thomas Garrett, an UGRR stationmaster who sheltered hundreds of fugitive slaves in his home in Wilmington, Delaware,

Reverend James Miller McKim, who hired William Still to work for the Pennsylvania Anti-Slavery Society

before sending them on to Philadelphia, twenty-five miles away. Pennsylvania Anti-Slavery Society officials Robert Purvis and James Miller McKim also became his friends. Purvis, whose Philadelphia home was a major UGRR station, was a target for bigots of all types, for he was of English, African, Muslim, and Jewish ancestry. McKim, a Presbyterian minister, edited the *Pennsylvania Freeman*, the Pennsylvania Anti-Slavery Society's newspaper, and also ran the society's office at 107 North Fifth Street.

An incident involving Samuel D. Burris of the Pennsylvania Anti-Slavery Society illustrated the danger of abolitionist work. Burris, a free black UGRR conductor, often journeyed into Delaware, which allowed slavery, to lead slaves north to freedom. Eventually he was caught and jailed in Dover, Delaware, for more than a year. His sentence for rescuing slaves was to be sold into slavery himself. James Miller McKim learned of this and arranged for an abolitionist friend to purchase him. At the sale the abolitionist outbid everyone, buying Samuel D. Burris for $500. As Burris was led away in chains, the buyer whispered in his ear: "Everything is all right. You have been bought with abolitionist

Samuel D. Burris, a black UGRR conductor who was nearly sold into slavery

gold." Burris was taken back to Philadelphia to rejoin the wife and children he had thought he would never see again. But having barely escaped spending the rest of his life in bondage, he gave up rescuing slaves and moved to California.

In the fall of 1847, James Miller McKim asked William if he would like to work for the Pennsylvania Anti-Slavery Society as a janitor and clerk. In an age when laborers typically earned $6 a week, the society could pay him a weekly salary of only $3.75, but William accepted, hoping that his responsibilities—and pay—would eventually expand.

Around the time that he began his new job, William met a young dressmaker named Letitia George at a Sunday school where he did volunteer work. William and Letitia fell in love and were married sometime in 1847. His small salary and her earnings from making dresses enabled the couple to buy their own home at 832 South Street.

Before long William was doing more than sweeping floors and filing papers at the Anti-Slavery Society Office. Reverend McKim was greatly impressed by William's enthusiasm and ability and introduced him to the society's inner workings. William learned that fugitive slaves were hidden in some unexpected places. For example, live runaways were sometimes smuggled out of the city in caskets, as if they were dead people. James Bias, a prominent doctor, treated sick and injured runaway slaves and sheltered them at the boardinghouse run by his wife and himself.

Soon William and Letitia Still were asked if they, too, would turn their home into an UGRR station. The couple eagerly agreed, and so, late at night, the Stills began hearing secret raps at their door and finding ragged-looking strangers at their entrance. The fugitives would stay with the Stills for a few days. If it seemed safe for the runaway slaves to remain in Philadelphia, William would give them a false name and help them find work. Otherwise they would be whisked away by wagon in the middle of the night, to be passed along by the UGRR to a safer haven farther north.

William quickly became a leader of the Anti-Slavery Society. Everyone saw that he was reliable, trustworthy, and completely dedicated to the cause. As the son of former slaves, he had a gift for talking to fugitives and putting them at ease. He also had a gentlemanly and polite manner that earned the respect of everyone he met. Within a short while another janitor was hired and William had taken over much of the day-to-day work of running the Anti-Slavery Society Office from Reverend McKim at a salary of $7 a week. According to some estimates, nineteen out of every twenty fugitive slaves who arrived in Philadelphia between about 1847 and 1861 came to William Still's home or were aided by him at the Pennsylvania Anti-Slavery Society Office.

William aided in some remarkable slave escapes. One involved Ellen and William Craft. A relatively light-skinned slave, Ellen dressed in men's clothes and pretended to be "Mr. Johnson," a rich white planter heading to Philadelphia. Her husband posed as "Mr. Johnson's" trusty slave. Despite numerous brushes with capture, the Crafts traveled a thousand miles by train and steamboat from Georgia, entering Philadelphia on Christmas morning of 1848. William Still helped hide the couple on a farm for three weeks. Then in early 1849 the Crafts were sent farther north to Boston.

Another noteworthy escape began in March of 1849 when UGRR worker Samuel Smith of Richmond, Virginia, sent Still a telegram saying that a "case of goods" would soon arrive in Philadelphia. In the UGRR's secret language, "goods," "articles," "packages," and "items" meant fugitive slaves. Smith packed a slave named Henry Brown into a crate that supposedly contained a shipment of shoes. For about thirty hours Henry was squashed inside the box, breathing through three little holes as he was transported by train and steamboat to Philadelphia. The box finally arrived in the Anti-Slavery Society Office where William Still, Reverend McKim, and two other men opened the lid. When the fugitive popped out of the crate, William Still and his colleagues nicknamed him "Box" Brown because of the way he had escaped.

The most famous of all UGRR conductors also visited William Still periodically. Following her escape from slavery in 1849, Harriet Tubman returned to the South many times. She led hundreds of slaves to freedom, sometimes bringing them to William Still's home or office.

By the summer of 1850, William Still had worked at the Pennsylvania Anti-Slavery Society for almost three years. Now twenty-eight years old, he had risen from janitor to become one of the society's most important members—probably *the* most indispensable member. As he later wrote, he had heard so many "sad and thrilling stories" of escaped slaves that the extraordinary had begun to seem ordinary to him. Day in and day out, he met slaves who had walked hundreds of miles through rain and snow, lived in caves for weeks at a time, and even breathed through reeds while hiding underwater to evade slave catchers.

But if William Still thought that he had seen everything, he was about to receive the shock of his life.

CHAPTER X

"Sir, I'd Like to Buy Myself"

Peter began 1848 with great hope. From doing odd jobs over the past few years, he now had $210 hidden in his leather pouch. Although he had lived a slave for nearly half a century, he felt that, if the Friedmans would aid him, he might yet be free.

On a January day Peter walked into the back room of the store, where Joseph Friedman was working on his account book. "Mr. Friedman," began Peter, his knees trembling so much that he could scarcely stand. "I've got something I want to tell you—but it's a great secret."

"Well, Peter?" asked Mr. Friedman.

For a few moments he couldn't seem to talk. Then he blurted out, "Sir—I'd like to buy myself. You've always dealt so fair with me, I didn't know but you might buy me, then give me a chance to buy myself from you."

As Joseph Friedman's face brightened, Peter nearly cried with happiness. "I have always hoped by some means you might be free," Mr. Friedman said, "but such a plan as this had not occurred to me."

Mr. Friedman said that it must appear to be a business deal—or both of them might be jailed for breaking Alabama's law about freeing slaves. There must be documents each step of the way as Mr. Friedman purchased Peter and then Peter bought himself.

Peter figured that the Hogun family could afford to sell him for $500. Mr. Friedman, thinking Peter would not go for less than $800, made a suggestion to lower his value. Whenever Peter was near Mr. Hogun, he should cough. Hogun might conclude that Peter was sick and be more likely to sell him.

Soon after his conversation with Peter, Joseph Friedman went to speak to John Henry Hogun, and offered him $500. Friedman added that, although Peter had a cough, he was willing to take him as is and try to cure it. Hogun refused the offer, saying Peter was worth twice that much. Joseph Friedman walked away disappointed, but not nearly as disappointed as Peter when he heard what had happened.

A few months later Joseph Friedman went to Texas to open another store. He left his brother Isaac in charge in Tuscumbia and instructed him to continue offering to buy Peter from Mr. Hogun. But Isaac Friedman had no more success than his older brother. Finally Peter visited his owner himself. Coughing mightily, Peter asked Hogun to accept Friedman's offer. But he refused, saying Peter was worth twice the $500 they offered. Besides, he had no intention of parting with him.

Peter walked back to Tuscumbia with a heavy heart. If John Henry Hogun refused to sell him, his dream of freedom might be lost forever. He could do only one thing, he decided: Keep putting away money and hope that eventually his owner would change his mind.

When 1848 came to a close, John Henry Hogun hired Peter out again to the Friedman brothers. By then Peter had about $300 in his purse, but what good was it if Mr. Hogun wouldn't sell him?

On January 10, 1849, something finally happened to change Hogun's mind. He wanted to buy two young slaves who were being auctioned in Tuscumbia but didn't have enough cash. Hogun called upon Isaac Friedman at his store to propose a deal.

After Mr. Hogun left the store, Isaac Friedman described the proposal to Peter. If Friedman went down the street to the auction house and purchased one of the slaves for him, Hogun would trade Peter to Friedman in return. Peter didn't like the idea. If the slave cost Mr. Friedman $800 or $1,000, then Peter would have to pay Isaac Friedman that much money to buy himself.

He advised Isaac Friedman to forget about the trade. Instead Mr. Friedman should renew his offer to buy Peter for $500. Mr. Hogun could then use the money to purchase the slave at the auction.

A few minutes later Hogun returned to the store to see what Isaac Friedman had decided. From the back room Peter overheard their conversation. He would not attend the auction, insisted Mr. Friedman. Then he repeated his offer to buy Peter from Hogun for $500.

Slave auction

The sale at the auction house had already begun, and Mr. Hogun was becoming desperate for the money. "Well," he said, "you may have him for five hundred, but it's a shame to sell him so."

Hogun spent the $500 he received for Peter to buy the young slave he wanted. Five days later Hogun drew up an official bill of sale regarding Peter:

$500. For the consideration of five hundred dollars, I have sold to Joseph Friedman a negro man named Peter. I bind myself and heirs to defend the title of said negro, Peter, to the said Joseph Friedman and his heirs against all claims whatever.

Given under my hand and seal this 15th day of January, 1849.

JOHN H. HOGUN

The first part of the plan had been accomplished. Peter was now the property of Joseph and Isaac Friedman. As the news spread, people in Tuscumbia extended their sympathy to Uncle Peter. The townspeople warned him that Jews were so greedy they would sell their own children and the Friedmans would probably sell him far away from his family. Peter thought to himself that these "greedy Jews" were the first people who had ever offered him a chance at freedom.

Isaac Friedman had another surprise for Peter. He would work in the store, as he had done before, but from now on the Friedmans would pay him wages and he could keep all his earnings. When he had $500, they would give him his free papers, and he could go where he liked. In other words, although technically the

---

Know all Men by these presents, *That*

do, by these presents, for good and valuable considerations, fully and absolutely *Manumit, make Free, and set at Liberty,*   slave, named
hereby willing and declaring that the said
shall and may, at all times hereafter, exercise, hold, and enjoy, all and singular the liberties, rights, privileges, and immunities of   free
fully to all intents and purposes, as if   had been born free.—And
do hereby, for   Executors, Administrators, and Assigns,
absolutely relinquish and release all   right, title, and property whatsoever,
in and to the said   as   slave.

IN TESTIMONY WHEREOF,   *have hereunto set   hand and seal, the*
day of   *one thousand eight hundred and*

SEALED AND DELIVERED IN
THE PRESENCE OF

Freedom papers; to free a slave, the master filled in the slave's name and other information.

Friedmans' property, Peter would be paid for his work and would not be treated like a slave.

On a Saturday night shortly after the Friedmans bought him, Peter visited his family. He was free—or *almost* free—he whispered to Vina and the children. Once he paid the Friedmans the $500, he would be a slave no more. Then he would head north to Philadelphia and search for his relatives. But—Peter solemnly promised his wife and children—he would find a way to free them, too. He would free them all if it was the last thing he did! They must keep his plan secret, Peter added, for if word got out that he was buying himself, he and the Friedmans might be thrown in jail.

He asked another thing of his children—something that might be difficult. At this time Vina and Peter's sons, Peter Jr., Levin, and William, were respectively twenty-two, nineteen, and seventeen years old. Only Catharine, who was about eleven, was not yet of marriageable age. They must try not to fall in love, Peter advised his sons and daughter. If they married and had children, it would be more difficult for Peter to rescue them all from slavery.

Just two weeks after the Friedmans purchased him, Peter removed his purse from its hiding place and handed $300 to Isaac Friedman. Mr. Friedman gave him a receipt and promised that, when Peter paid $200 more, he would receive his free papers. Peter figured he would need only a year and a half to save the remaining money, for now that the Friedmans were paying him for his work, he was saving more than $10 a month.

Everything seemed to be going smoothly for Peter.

Sometime before mid-1849 Peter and Vina's third son, William, was hired out as a house slave to a Captain Bell in Tuscumbia. Peter was happy to have William in the same town where he worked, and father and son arranged for their paths to cross often as they ran errands around Tuscumbia.

On a hot Sunday in July, Captain Bell allowed William to go fishing outside of town on Spring Creek. In the afternoon several of his friends found William's clothes on the bank, but there was no sign of William. The boys ran into Tuscumbia to report what had happened.

Word was sent to Peter and Vina that their son had disappeared. Peter rushed to Spring Creek and joined the crowd that was searching the water. Eventually William's lifeless body was found at the bottom of the creek. The grieving father carried his dead son back to Vina's cabin in a wagon. That night, by torchlight, Peter and Vina buried their youngest son near the resting places of their four children who had died in infancy.

The death of their son devastated Peter and Vina, but it did not end their quest for liberty. Peter was all the more determined that his wife and three remaining children would be free.

In the fall of 1849, Joseph Friedman returned from Texas. He was pleased by all that had happened and congratulated Peter on his prospect of soon being liberated. On September 1 Peter paid the Friedmans another $100. Now only the final $100 separated him from freedom.

But as the great moment neared, Peter had another worry. How would he get out of Alabama? If he traveled by himself, authorities might arrest him for being freed contrary to Alabama law. And even if he got out of Alabama, how could he pass through other slave states such as Tennessee and Kentucky? The Friedman brothers devised a plan. In a few months they were going to sell their store and leave Alabama. Gold had recently been discovered in California. Joseph Friedman wanted to join the forty-niners flocking to the gold rush. Isaac, however, was moving to Cincinnati, Ohio, to join another brother in business, and he would take Peter with him. Once in the Free State of Ohio, Peter would be safe.

In March of 1850 Peter paid Joseph Friedman $60 more. Now only $40 from freedom, he worked all hours of the night at every odd job he could find. On a glorious spring day, he counted and recounted his coins to make certain he wasn't mistaken.

He had the final $40.

Late on the evening of April 16, 1850, Peter entered the back room of the store. His legs and hands trembled, as they had a year and three months earlier when he had first asked Joseph Friedman to buy him. What if all this was just a trick and the Friedmans never intended to grant him his freedom? What if, instead of giving him his free papers, they sold him farther south, as had happened to Spencer, the stable man in Lexington, Kentucky, so many years earlier?

Joseph Friedman looked up from his account book and smiled at Peter. Timidly Peter withdrew his leather purse from his pocket, untied the string, and poured his coins onto the desk. Mr. Friedman was in the midst of counting the money when suddenly the bell on the door jingled and someone entered the store. Mr. Friedman covered Peter's coins with a pile of papers, but it was too late. A businessman from down the street had walked into the back room and noticed the money.

Fortunately the man assumed that Peter was paying Friedman a percentage of the money he had earned from doing odd jobs around town. The neighbor said good-bye and left the store. When they heard his footsteps fading in the distance, Peter and Joseph Friedman resumed their counting. Yes, Joseph Friedman said, this was the final $40. So excited he was afraid he might faint, Peter waited as Mr. Friedman wrote out a receipt and a paper that, he explained, was a Certificate of Freedom. After completing the papers, Mr. Friedman handed Peter his copies:

Received, Tuscumbia, January 26th,
1849, of my boy Peter,
three hundred dollars $300.00

Recd. Sept. 1st, 1849, of my boy Peter,
eighty-eight dollars and twelve dollars $100.00

Recd. March 29th, 1850, of Peter,
sixty dollars $60.00
                                                          _____
                                                           $460.00

Received, April 16th, 1850, forty dollars $40.00

————————
$500.00

For, and in consideration of the above five hundred dollars, I have this 16th day of April, 1850, given Peter a Bill of Sale, and given him his freedom.

JOSEPH FRIEDMAN
Tuscumbia, Ala., April 16th, 1850

Although Peter couldn't read, over the years he had learned to recognize a few words. The most beautiful word he had ever seen was the one Joseph Friedman had written before he signed his name: *freedom*. As Peter stared at the word at the bottom of the paper, it slowly sank in. After fifty years in slavery, he was free.

He offered Joseph Friedman his gratitude and shook his hand. Probably he cried. Then Peter placed the precious papers in his purse and walked out into the spring night—a free man.

CHAPTER XI

"I WILL COME BACK!"

Afew days after Peter paid his last $40, Joseph Friedman headed for California. Apparently he lived there only a short while and then moved to Detroit, Michigan, where he became a dry-goods merchant and helped found the city's first Jewish synagogue.

Peter remained in Tuscumbia with Isaac Friedman for three more months. He used the time to save money for his trip to the North, for he had only $6 left after buying himself.

Isaac Friedman concocted a story that he and Peter spread around Tuscumbia. Isaac claimed that he was temporarily closing the Tuscumbia store and taking Peter with him to Cincinnati, Ohio, for a visit. He and Peter would return to Tuscumbia in a few months and reopen the store. Hearing that, white Tuscumbians pointed out Uncle Peter as an example to other slaves. Peter was so faithful, they said, that he could visit a Free State with his master and be counted on to return home. "What a contented old fellow he is!" Peter overheard a man say. "I'd like the abolitionists to hear him talk. They would be obliged to admit that slaves' pining to be free is just moonshine!"

On Saturday night, July 13, 1850, Peter made a farewell visit to his family. It was a bittersweet weekend, for, despite Peter's assertions that he would free them, too, his wife and children knew that many things might prevent this. On Monday morning, as the bell rang calling Vina, Peter Jr., Levin, and Catharine to work, the family knew that this might be their last time together.

Peter walked his wife and children outside. His tearful sons and daughter said their good-byes and headed toward the cotton field. Vina climbed onto her mule and rode slowly toward the field as Peter walked by her side. Peter told his wife not to worry about him and assured her that one day they would be together in a happier land. Then the moment came for them to part.

"Well, Peter," said Vina, "this here's your road, and yonder's mine. Good-bye!"

Peter stared into his wife's eyes. "I will come back!" he promised her. "Whether I find my people or not in Philadelphia, I will come back! Now take care of yourself and the children, and mind they don't tell the secret."

Peter pressed Vina's hand one more time. Finally he let go and set off down the road to Tuscumbia.

✧ ✧ ✧

Peter promising Vina that he will come back for her and the children

The following Saturday, July 20, 1850, Isaac Friedman and Peter went to the landing. While they awaited the steamboat's arrival, a doctor from Tuscumbia took Peter aside. "Mind what I tell you," he said. "If those Jews decide to sell you, just telegraph to me."

"Thank you, sir, I will," Peter answered, "but I reckon they ain't gonna sell me anyhow."

Soon the *Greek Slave* arrived, and the white storekeeper and the black ex-slave boarded the vessel. They steamed along the Tennessee River to where it emptied into the Ohio River at Paducah, Kentucky, and from there they traveled up the Ohio. At six o'clock on the morning of July 26, 1850, they docked at Cincinnati, Ohio.

Peter was too excited to wait for the gangplank. He leaped over the railing to the ground, clapping his hands and shouting: "I'm free! I'm *free!* This is free ground! The water runs free! The wind blows free! I am a slave no more!"

Isaac Friedman took Peter with him to the home of some relatives. Peter told the Friedmans the story of his life, explaining that he was going to Philadelphia to search for his kinfolk.

Isaac Friedman did not like sending Peter on alone. Cholera was raging on the river, and he might get sick and die among strangers. There was another danger, Isaac warned. The Ohio River was a major dividing line between the slave states and Free States. White men traveled along the river looking for free black people like Peter to kidnap and sell back into slavery.

But Peter wouldn't be stopped now that he had a chance of finding his long-lost family.

After a day and a half in Cincinnati, Peter returned to the wharf and boarded a steamboat bound for Pittsburgh, Pennsylvania. Soon Isaac Friedman's warning came to mind. As the vessel steamed up the Ohio River, Peter noticed two or three passengers staring at him in a manner that made him uncomfortable.

A short, sour-looking man asked Peter if his owner was on board. Peter could have pulled his free papers out of his pocket and proven that he wasn't a slave. But if the man grabbed the papers and threw them over the railing, Peter would have no evidence that he was free.

"I don't have any owner!" Peter answered, and walked away.

Next an elderly gentleman approached Peter and asked the same question.

"I have no master!" Peter repeated with annoyance, for he knew that the way to convince people he was free was to act like a free man. "Who said I had a master?"

"But you are a slave," persisted the elderly gentleman, "or at least you have been one. I knew it as soon as I saw you. Where are you going?"

"I am going to Pittsburgh, and then to Philadelphia, and I am a free man!" Peter insisted. "Who said I had a master?"

Two black barbers on the boat informed Peter that he had nothing to worry about from the elderly gentleman. The short, sour-looking man was a different story. He was a detective and was telling people that, if he weren't hunting a man who had escaped prison, he would capture Peter, whom he believed to be a runaway slave.

As the boat approached Wheeling, Virginia (now in West Virginia), several people came up to Peter to advise him. One man pressed a five-dollar gold piece into his hand and told him he was a friend to colored people. He urged Peter to get off at Wheeling and walk across the bridge to the Free State of Ohio.

Peter suspected that this fellow and the sour-faced man were plotting to capture him. If he got off at Wheeling, Peter knew, he would be in the slave state of Virginia, where he might be seized and sold back into bondage. Peter returned the gold piece to the man with thanks. He had paid his passage to Pittsburgh, and he would not leave the boat until then.

Despite his brave front, Peter was extremely worried. He was free, yet one wrong move could mean that he would spend the rest of his days a slave.

Early the next morning the boat reached Pittsburgh, Pennsylvania. A black man Peter had met on the vessel took him to the home of a friend, where Peter had breakfast and was given some useful information. Once in Philadelphia, he could stay in a boardinghouse run by a black couple named Dr. and Mrs. Bias.

Five hours after arriving in Pittsburgh, Peter went to the city's stagecoach station. He bought a ticket that was supposed to allow him to ride inside the vehicle. The stagecoach was crowded with white passengers, however, so, even in the Free State of Pennsylvania, he was told to sit outside with the driver.

East of Pittsburgh they entered the Allegheny Mountains. As he looked at the peaks, Peter thought about his wife and children in Alabama. How strange it seemed that the same sun sparkling so beautifully through the Pennsylvania mountains was at that very moment beating down upon his loved ones in the Alabama cotton fields.

After a stagecoach ride of about twenty-four hours, Peter boarded a train. Back home in Alabama there had been a rickety train pulled by a few mules, but this was the first locomotive he had ever seen. He stared out the window in astonishment as the train roared past villages and farms. On the afternoon of Thursday, August 1, 1850, the train blasted its whistle. Through the window Peter beheld the largest town he had ever seen. He had arrived in Philadelphia after a twelve-day, fifteen-hundred-mile journey by steamboat, stagecoach, and train.

He picked up the trunk the Friedmans had provided and stepped off the train. Porters were scurrying about the platform, asking people where they wanted their bags carried. A porter approached him, but Peter couldn't remember the name of the people who owned the boardinghouse where he had been advised to go. He stood by his trunk for half an hour, until all the other passengers were gone. Finally an elderly black man approached him and asked Peter if he were lost.

Peter told him about the boardinghouse that had been recommended to him in Pittsburgh. The elderly black man mentioned many names, but none sounded right to Peter. Then the man said the name Dr. Bias, and Peter knew that was the man.

The elderly man was a porter. He told Peter he knew the address and would take him there for a quarter. Peter readily agreed.

The man placed the trunk upon his shoulder and set out through the Philadelphia streets. Peter followed, staring at every black person he passed in hope of seeing someone who resembled his parents or two sisters. The elderly man carried the trunk to the Bias boardinghouse, where Peter thanked him and paid him the quarter.

Mrs. Bias answered the door, explaining to Peter that her husband, Dr. James Bias, was away in Cincinnati. He had just come from there, Peter said, and on the way he had been advised to come to the Biases for help. "Come in," said Mrs. Bias, offering to provide him shelter.

Peter sat in the parlor and tried to listen while Mrs. Bias described what her husband was doing in Cincinnati. But he was deep in thought and wasn't paying much attention. Suddenly he asked if she knew how far it was to the Delaware River.

Mrs. Bias pointed toward the wharfs.

Peter sprang to his feet. He explained that he was going off to try and learn what had become of his parents and two sisters, whom he hadn't seen in about forty-five years. He recounted how he and his brother Levin had been stolen away from their home in Maryland, and how he believed the rest of his family had settled near the Delaware River around Philadelphia.

Over the years Mrs. Bias and her husband had sheltered many runaway slaves. Although she realized that Peter was no fugitive, she also knew that he had no idea what he was undertaking. Philadelphia and the nearby towns along the Delaware River in Pennsylvania and New Jersey contained thousands of people, Mrs. Bias explained. It would be difficult to find his relatives—even if any of them were alive and living nearby.

Peter still wanted to start looking for his family at once.

Mrs. Bias admired the fortitude of a man who would wait forty-five years for freedom, travel fifteen hundred miles, then go searching for his relatives within an hour of his arrival. She convinced him to stay a few minutes to eat lunch, or dinner as people called it in those days. Then she led him to the river, repeating her street address several times so that he could find his way back.

For several hours Peter explored neighborhoods along the river, asking every black person he met if they knew of an elderly couple named Levin and Cidney who had lost two children more than forty years earlier. No one had heard of the couple, but in his wanderings Peter began to understand how big Philadelphia was. He realized that it might take many such explorations before he discovered anything.

Later in the afternoon Peter returned to the boardinghouse. Touched by his plight, Mrs. Bias sent a friend of hers to help him in his search. Accompanied by this man, Peter went out again. They walked the streets near the river until well after dark, when Peter again returned to Mrs. Bias's.

At dawn Peter arose and went out to continue his search. One old man he met had lived in Philadelphia for fifty-three years, yet he had never known former slaves named Levin and Cidney. By the time he returned to Mrs. Bias in the late afternoon, Peter thought he would have to widen his search to include nearby towns, including those on the New Jersey side of the river.

Perhaps something about Peter's face gave Mrs. Bias an idea. In the evening she once again sent for the guide who had accompanied Peter the previous day. She told the man to take Peter to the Pennsylvania Anti-Slavery Society Office at 107 North Fifth Street. At about six o'clock in the evening, Peter and Mrs. Bias's friend headed to the Anti-Slavery Society's headquarters.

When they reached the office, Peter looked through the window and saw a young black man writing at a desk. The guide asked Peter if he'd ever seen a black man doing that in the South. Peter told him that, if a black man there knew how to write, he'd best keep it a secret.

They entered the office and the man at the desk, who was sending out the weekly issue of the *Pennsylvania Freeman*, put down his pen. Peter observed that he was neatly dressed, with friendly, caring eyes.

"Good evening, Mr. Still," said Peter's guide. "Here is a man from the South who says he is hunting for his people. Mrs. Bias sent me here with him. She thought you might possibly know what had become of his relatives."

Peter and Mr. Still stared at each other as they shook hands. This young man's face, thought Peter, resembled his brother Levin, who had died nineteen years earlier. Something about this old fellow, thought William Still, reminded him of his mother and his brother James.

"What were the names of your mother and father?" Mr. Still asked Peter.

"My father's name was Levin, and my mother's name was Cidney, and we had two sisters, Mahalah and Kitturah," said Peter. "One day when our mother was gone—we thought to church—a white man come along and asked my brother Levin and me if we didn't want to ride in his gig. He told us he would carry us to our mother, so we got up with him. But he took us off into Kentucky and sold us. We used to talk a heap about our mother, but nineteen years ago my brother died in Alabama. And now I've bought my liberty and come back to hunt for my relations."

Astounded by what he had heard, William Still demanded more information. "What was the name of your parents' owner in Maryland?"

"Saunders Griffin," answered Peter.

William Still was so shaken he had to sit down. "Suppose I should tell you that I am your brother?" he asked.

Peter doubted that Mr. Still, despite his resemblance to Levin, was really his brother. He was about twenty years younger than Peter. Moreover, Peter was so worried about slave catchers that he feared Mr. Still might be part of a plot to seize him and return him to bondage.

"Supposing you should?" Peter said doubtfully.

"Well," continued Mr. Still, "from all you have told me, I believe you are a brother of mine. My father's name was Levin, and my mother's name is Cidney. And they lost two boys named Levin and Peter about the time you speak of. I have often heard my mother mourn about those two lost children, and I am sure you must be one of them."

As he spoke, Mr. Still's voice trembled, and he seemed to be close to tears. But Peter was still suspicious, for all the young man had done was repeat Peter's story. He asked William if his parents were living. Surely his own parents must be long dead, but Peter hoped to find their graves. Mr. Still explained that his father was dead, but his mother was still alive.

In the midst of the conversation, the guide rose to depart. Peter was afraid to be left alone in what might be a nest of kidnappers. But before Peter could follow him, the guide went out the door and Mr. Still said that he would take Peter back to Mrs. Bias's.

Then suddenly Mr. Still changed his mind about taking Peter to Mrs. Bias's. "Come with me to my sister's," he said. "One of them lives quite near. She is several years older than I and can tell you much more about our family."

Peter did not want to be roaming about this dangerous city at night with a complete stranger, and he asked to be taken to his boardinghouse.

William Still couldn't bear to let Peter, who he was certain was his brother, get away. Philadelphia could be a dangerous place for a black man unfamiliar with the city's ways. What if slave catchers seized Peter before he was able to meet the rest of his family? Yes, he would take him to Mrs. Bias's, Mr. Still promised, but first he would be most grateful if Peter would come meet his sister Mary, an unmarried schoolteacher. Mr. Still was so insistent that Peter was unable to refuse.

When William arrived with Peter at her house,

Mary Still was just finishing her tea. Assuming the stranger was another of the fugitive slaves her brother often brought home with him, Mary hardly gave Peter a glance.

"Sister," said William, "here is a man who tells a strange story. He has come to Philadelphia to look for his relations, and I should like to have you hear what he has to say."

Mary Still, who appeared to Peter to be about forty years old, looked at him for the first time. "For whom are you looking?" she asked.

"Oh," Peter told her, "I'm a-looking for a needle in a haystack, and I reckon the needle's rusty and the stack's rotted down, so it's no use saying any more about it."

"But tell her," insisted Mr. Still, "what you related to me in the office."

Peter began his story, but when he said, "My father's name was Levin, and my mother's name was Cidney—" Mary Still leaped out of her chair. Seizing a candle, she held it near Peter's face and studied his every feature. "Oh, Lord!" she cried. "It is one of our lost brothers! I should know him by his likeness to our mother. Thank God! One of our brothers has come!" Then she turned to Mr. Still and said, "Oh, William, this will kill Mother!"

The way she said *this will kill Mother!* momentarily convinced Peter that these two people truly were his sister and brother. Then he caught himself, for his heart had been broken too many times for him to believe a story like this without more proof.

Mary Still implored Peter to return in the morning

and go with her to see an older sister who lived in another part of Philadelphia. Peter agreed. Then, as he had promised, William Still walked Peter back to his boardinghouse.

"Good evening, Mrs. Bias," said William Still, entering her parlor with Peter. "Did you send this man to the Anti-Slavery Society Office this evening?"

"Yes, sir," Mrs. Bias answered, looking from one brother to the other. "I thought he might find some account there of his people."

"Well, he is my own brother!" said William. "My parents lost two children more than forty years ago. And from this man's story I am convinced that he is one of those brothers. And now I have brought him back here, as I promised at the office. But I want him to go home with me and stay the night. In the morning I will take him to see other members of our family."

"No, sir," said Peter, "I'd as lief stay here tonight, and then I can go with you in the morning."

Pointing out that they really did look like brothers, Mrs. Bias urged Peter to go with Mr. Still. Peter hesitated, but William persuaded him by promising that, if he came along, he would get to see his mother in a day or two.

Peter walked with William Still to a three-story brick house in a pleasant and quiet neighborhood. His wife, Letitia, was away, William explained. She was in New Jersey visiting some of William's relatives—rather William *and Peter's* relatives. Peter ate supper with William, who then showed him to a bedroom.

Once alone, Peter burst into tears. Could it be that, after nearly forty-five years, his dear mother lived? Or would he be seized during the night and sold where Vina and his children would never see him again? He looked under the bed and inside the closet to make sure no one was hiding in the room. Then he piled furniture in front of the door to block anyone from coming in during the night. He lay down to a troubled sleep, dreaming that armed men had entered the room to grab him.

After breakfast the next morning, William Still walked Peter back to Mary's house. He wanted to spend this day with Peter, William said, but he had some important business at the Anti-Slavery Society Office. William departed, leaving Peter with Mary. Peter's fears eased somewhat. Surely Mary wouldn't consent to be alone with him unless she truly believed he was her brother.

Mary led Peter to the home of the other sister who lived in Philadelphia. Her name was Kitty and she was a widow, Mary informed him. Kitty's daughter answered the door. The moment she saw Peter, the daughter cried, "Oh, Mother, Aunt Mary has brought a man with her that looks just like my grandfather. Come, quick, and see him!"

Once inside, Mary said, "Kitty, here is one of our lost brothers. He came to William last night, and I am taking him to see Mother!"

Looking at Peter, Kitty seemed to know without doubt that he was her brother. "I'll go, too!" Kitty said with tremendous excitement. "How glad I am, but what will Mother say?"

As Peter stared back at Kitty, he wondered, Could she be his sister Kitturah? She had been a very little girl when he had last seen her, and he couldn't tell for sure.

That afternoon Peter accompanied Mary and Kitty to the wharf and boarded a Delaware River steamboat. The two women kept asking him questions and saying how happy they were to find him, and as he listened and spoke with them, his last doubts melted away. He had found his sisters! His mother was alive, and soon he would once more look upon her dear face!

Before visiting their mother they would stop in Medford, New Jersey, to see their brother James Still, explained Peter's sisters. They traveled about ten miles along the river to a place called Long Bridge, where they boarded a stagecoach.

"There is brother James walking by the barn," said one of Peter's sisters, when they arrived at his house in Medford.

As James approached them, Peter was struck by the family resemblance. He felt that he had gone back twenty years and was looking at his brother Levin.

That night Peter sat by the fireplace with his sisters Mary and Kitty and his brother James, an unlicensed physician known as the *Doctor of the Pines*. Peter recounted his and Levin's lives, and told them about his wife and children, who remained slaves in Alabama.

Early the next morning the two brothers and two sisters set out in James's carriage for the home of their mother, who lived about ten miles away on a farm with her son Samuel. On the way, his sisters warned Peter that their mother was frail, and might not survive the shock if he revealed his identity too suddenly.

An elderly woman was standing in the doorway when the carrriage pulled up to the farmhouse early on that morning of Sunday, August 4, 1850. Several of her children usually visited her on Sunday, so Charity had been looking out for them.

Seeing his mother in the doorway, Peter wanted to leap from the wagon and run to her, but his sisters' warning was fresh in his ears. He restrained himself and stood aside as James, Mary, and Kitty went up to their mother and politely kissed her.

The group entered the parlor, where Peter took a seat near his mother. Her vision was poor, so he stared at her face without her seeming to notice. How different she looked from the mother he remembered. But there, on one side of her face, was the mole that he and Levin had argued about so often.

After James, Kitty, and Mary had spoken to their mother awhile, Peter commented, "You have a large family."

"Yes," his mother replied, trying to get a better look at him, "I have had eighteen children."

"How many have you living?" Peter asked.

"I have buried eight," she answered, "and I have eight living."

"I thought you said you had eighteen—eight living and eight dead would make but sixteen," said Peter.

His mother sighed and said, "Ahh! I've grieved about them two lost boys a great many years."

"What became of them?" Peter continued.

"I never knew what became of them. I left them asleep in bed the last time I saw them. I never knew whether they was stole and carried off or they was dead."

Just then another of her children, Mahalah, rushed in. The last time Peter had seen her, Mahalah had been perhaps three years old, and he remembered her face. "Do tell me," cried Mahalah, out of breath, "what is the matter? Is anybody dead?" Glancing around the room she noticed Peter. "Who's this?" Mahalah asked. "Who is he? Isn't he one of Mother's lost children? He favors the family, and I'm sure he must be one of them."

His mother leaned over to look closely at Peter's face. She stared at him a long time. Then she rose slowly and walked into another room, where she knelt in prayer.

In a few minutes she returned, her whole body trembling. "Who are you?" she asked Peter.

"My name is Peter," he said gently, "and I had a brother Levin."

"Oh, Lord," cried his mother, clasping Peter to her heart, "how long have I prayed to see my two sons! Can it be that they have come?"

For a long while the mother and son stood holding each other with tears flowing down their cheeks.

CHAPTER XII

"I WOULD RATHER DIE THAN NOT GO BACK!"

William Still was profoundly moved by finding his lost brother and informed James Miller McKim about it. Reverend McKim asked William to make a record of his extraordinary meeting with his brother. Six days after first encountering Peter, William described the incident in a letter that Reverend McKim published in the *Pennsylvania Freeman* of August 22, 1850.

Anti-Slavery Office
Philadelphia
August 8th, 1850

MR. J. M. McKIM

Dear Sir:
    As you desired that I should make a statement of some of the most prominent facts in relation to the late wonderful discovery of one of my lost brothers, I submit the following brief account.

On the 2nd, two men came into this office, one of whom I recognized, the other was an entire stranger. My acquaintance introduced the stranger to me by the name of Peter Friedman, of Alabama. . . . Peter commenced his own story in an earnest and simple manner. . . . His visit here was for the purpose of seeing if he could gain some information how he might find his people. He stated that he and an older brother had been stolen away, about 41 or 42 years ago, when he was a boy only about six years old. Since that time he had been utterly excluded from all knowledge of his parents, having never heard a word from them or any of his relatives. . . . I then inquired of him if he knew the names of his parents. To which he replied that his father's name was Levin and his mother's Cidney; he did not know their last names. I was much surprised and interested at the remarks made by the stranger, and I continued to put such questions to him as I thought would, most likely, throw light upon the subject. . . .

By this time I perceived that a most wonderful story was about to be disclosed . . . and the fact was [soon] confirmed to my satisfaction, that an own dear brother whom I had never before seen was before me. There was no evading the evidence. All the names and the circumstances were familiar to me, having heard my parents speak of them very frequently. Besides, I could see in the face of my newfound brother the likeness of my mother. My feelings were unutterable. . . . I told him that

I could tell him all about his kinfolks. At this expression he seemed surprised, but not at all excited. I continued by telling him that he was an own brother of mine. . . .

He had endured the burdens of slavery with all its ills for forty-three long years, yet he had not yielded his hopes of . . . again greeting that mother who gave him birth. The distance he traveled was about 1,500 miles.

I shall not attempt to describe the feelings of my mother and the family on learning that Peter was one of us. I will leave that for you to imagine. You are probably aware that my father has been dead for seven years. Unfortunately brother Peter has a wife and three children in slavery. He has gone back to Alabama with the earnest hope of being able to liberate his wife and children. . . .

WM. STILL

His "wonderful discovery of my lost brother" changed the way William Still ran the Anti-Slavery Society Office. Like other UGRR workers, he had generally put nothing in writing about fugitive slaves for fear that his notes would fall into slave hunters' hands and be used to recapture the runaways. Now he realized that, if he gathered detailed information from fugitives he met, he might help reunite other families separated by slavery. Many years later, in the preface to his book *The Underground Railroad*, he explained:

The writer [William Still], in common with others [UGRR workers], took no notes. But after the restoration of Peter Still, his own brother, after forty years' cruel separation from his mother, and the wonderful discovery and joyful reunion, the idea forced itself upon his mind that all over this wide country thousands of mothers and children, separated by Slavery, were in a similar way living without the slightest knowledge of each other's where-abouts, praying and weeping without ceasing, as did this mother and son. Under these reflections it seemed reasonable to hope that by carefully gathering the narratives of Under-ground Railroad passengers, in some way or other some of the bleeding and severed hearts might be united and comforted.

William began writing down the narratives of fugitive slaves he assisted. He also wrote from memory the stories of fugitives he had previously aided, such as Henry "Box" Brown and Ellen and Willliam Craft. He stored his records in a place known only to him-self and perhaps a few other people: a building in Philadelphia's black-owned Lebanon Cemetery. Late at night William would make his way among the graves, climb up into the building's loft, and hide his notes in his secret location.

For a week Peter Still (for he had adopted his newfound family's last name) visited with his mother, brothers, and sisters. He was happy to be with his siblings and proud of their accomplishments, yet he couldn't help feeling jealous of their nice homes and jobs, their education, and especially their life as free blacks. He later admitted thinking to himself that slavery had kept him ignorant and poor, but times would change, and if ever he got his family, his children would have a chance to know as much as other people.

After Peter had spent a few days with his relatives, William asked him if he planned to live in Philadelphia permanently. Peter's answer shocked him: He was returning to Alabama to find a way to free his wife and children. William tried to change his mind. Fugitives commonly fantasized about returning to the South and rescuing their loved ones from slavery. The few who actually did it, such as Harriet Tubman, usually traveled a short way to places like Delaware and Maryland. Returning to a Deep South state like Alabama to rescue his family was impossible, William insisted. Most likely, the scheme would be uncovered, and Peter would be locked in an Alabama jail for trying to rescue slaves and for being illegally liberated himself.

Peter listened politely, then answered, "I would as soon go out of the world and die as not go back and do all I can for my family!"

His sisters, Mary, Kitturah, and Mahalah, and his brothers James and Samuel also begged him to reconsider. Not even his mother's pleas could change Peter's mind. On August 8, 1850—the same day William wrote his letter to the *Pennsylvania Freeman*—Peter Still set out to retrace his fifteen-hundred-mile journey. He had been in Philadelphia just one week.

He left Philadelphia by train, traveled by stagecoach over the Alleghenies, then returned by steamboat to Cincinnati. There he visited Isaac Friedman, his former owner, now his friend. Like Peter's brother William, Isaac was astounded at his plan to return to the South to try and liberate his wife and children. Isaac did what he could to assist Peter. He took him to visit Cincinnati Mayor Henry Spencer, who issued a paper stating that Peter was a free man:

> *State of Ohio*
> *City of Cincinnati*
> *Be it known that before me, Henry E. Spencer, Mayor of said City, personally appeared Isaac S. Friedman, who being duly sworn, deposes and says: that he has been acquainted with a colored man named Peter Still, alias Peter Friedman, for the last five years: that the said Peter was formerly a slave belonging to John H. Hogun, residing about three miles from Tuscumbia, in the State of Alabama: that Joseph Friedman, of Tuscumbia, hired the said Peter for about two years of the said John H. Hogun, and afterwards bought him, and held him as a slave for about two years longer, when Peter bought his freedom from his master, the said Joseph Friedman, brother of this deponent, by paying him the sum of five hundred dollars; as fully appears from a bill of sale given by said Joseph Friedman to said Peter, and dated Tuscumbia, Ala., the 16th day of April, 1850.*

I therefore do declare the above-named Peter Still, alias Peter Friedman, to be a free person, and entitled to all the privileges of free persons of color, according to the laws of the State of Ohio.

Said Peter Still is about forty-nine years of age, is five feet seven and a half inches in height, of a brownish black complexion, and without any marks or cuts.

Given under my hand, and the Corporate Seal of the City of Cincinnati, this 22nd day of August, 1850.

H. E. Spencer,
Mayor

This Certificate of Freedom declared that Ohio recognized Peter as a free man. If Alabama officials tried to re-enslave him because the Friedmans had liberated him without announcing it in a newspaper or applying to a judge, Peter could show them this paper. Alabama might be reluctant to argue with Ohio over the fact that the law hadn't been precisely followed when Peter had been freed.

Actually, Mayor Spencer's paper was likely to do Peter more harm than good.

White Alabamians did not want former slaves to remain in their state and influence friends and relatives who were still in bondage. The 1834 law making it difficult to free a slave also ordered that emancipated slaves leave Alabama "never more to return." In addition, it had a little-known "Penalty of Slave for Returning" clause, which stated:

If the [freed] slave or slaves shall return within the limits of this State, after such removal and emancipation, he, she, or they shall be subject to be apprehended by the sheriff of the county within which the [former slaves] may be found and imprisoned; and after having advertised the [former slaves] for at least thirty days, may be sold to the best bidder for cash, as slaves for life. . . .

Peter was in more danger than he or any of his friends and family realized. If he were forced to prove that he had been liberated, the "Penalty of Slave for Returning" clause might be invoked against him. The sheriff could arrest and imprison him for having returned to Alabama, and a month later Peter could be auctioned to the highest bidder.

The steamboat trip from Cincinnati to Tuscumbia was uneventful, for black people were bothered when heading *north*, not *south*. On the night of August 31, the vessel docked at Tuscumbia. Early on the first of September—a Sunday—Peter walked into town.

He saw many people he knew, and they all asked him why he had returned alone. Peter had a story ready that Isaac Friedman had made up for him. Master Isaac had sent Peter ahead to do odd jobs around town. In November Peter would deliver whatever money he earned to Mr. Friedman in Cincinnati. Then in December Mr. Friedman and Peter would return to Tuscumbia to reopen the store. Fortunately the story worked. So faithful was Uncle Peter, marveled white Tuscumbians, that his owner

When away from home, slaves had to show passes to white men who patrolled the roads.

could send him alone back and forth between Alabama and the free soil of Ohio!

Peter was eager to see his family, but he didn't want to raise suspicions by visiting them his first day back in town. For a day or two he went about Tuscumbia looking for employment. He was hired as janitor at the Tuscumbia Female Seminary, and also resumed running errands and doing odd jobs. He worked all week, then on Saturday night, September 7, he set out for Vina's cabin.

As he rode the twelve miles on a borrowed horse, Peter worried about what he would find. Was anyone sick? Had his wife, daughter, or one of his sons been sold? By the time he reached the Bernard McKiernan plantation, it was dark. He approached the cabin he had built for Vina twenty-five years earlier and peeked through the window. There were his wife and daughter, preparing supper. His sons were making a fire. *Thank God!* Peter said to himself. *They all live!*

His family rushed up to him the moment he entered the cabin. "Oh, Vina!" he said, holding his wife by both hands, "I've found my people! I've seen my mother, Vina! My mother's living, and I've got five brothers and three sisters!"

Peter told his wife and children everything that had occurred during the past seven weeks: his trip to Philadelphia, meeting his brother William, and the reunion with his mother. They asked again and again what freedom was like, and listened eagerly as he repeated his vow to liberate them, too.

For two and a half months, Peter remained in Tuscumbia, visiting his wife and children once every two weeks, as had been his custom. Gradually he realized that his brother William had been right—he would not be able to lead them to freedom himself. Unlike Peter, they had no free papers and, if stopped and questioned, would certainly be seized as runaway slaves.

Yet he could make a start at freeing them. One Sunday he crossed paths with Mrs. McKiernan, wife of the man who owned Vina and his children. "Mrs. McKiernan," Peter asked. "Master Isaac says he'll buy my family if I keep doing well working for him. Do you reckon Master McKiernan would sell them, ma'am?"

"I don't know," she replied. "He thinks a great deal of them all, and I reckon he would ask a high price for them. I don't believe less than three thousand dollars would buy them all, if indeed he would consent to let them go at all."

Peter revealed his plans to his wife and children. He would remain in Alabama until November. Then he would return to Philadelphia and raise the $3,000 to free them. It was a very large sum, he knew, but perhaps his brothers and sisters would lend him a portion of the money. Once Vina and the children were free and working in the North, they would repay the loan. Peter added that he had also heard some talk about sending a white abolitionist to Alabama to lead his loved ones to freedom. A white man might succeed at taking them away because everyone would assume he was just traveling northward with his slaves.

On Saturday, November 9, Peter rode his borrowed horse to the McKiernan plantation for his last visit with his family. He repeated his plan to purchase their freedom if possible and told them to be ready in case a man from the North came to take them away. "You'd best not marry," he reminded his children, "for if I live, I will get you all free, sure. And be good and kind to your mother, for she has no one now but you."

Before Peter departed, Vina gave him the cotton cape she was wearing and showed him that it had a hole in one corner. If a rescuer came for them, said Vina, he should bring the cape with him to prove that he was sent by Peter.

Monday morning arrived, and once more it was time for Peter to say good-bye to his family. He could tell that his sons and daughter truly believed that he would free them. But Vina cried, fearful that she would never see him again.

Peter kissed his wife and pressed her hands. Then he mounted his horse and rode back to Tuscumbia.

Entitled *"Effects of the Fugitive-Slave Law,"* this picture published
in 1850 shows fleeing slaves being pursued.

CHAPTER XIII

"MY FAMILY SHALL BE FREE!"

On November 13 Peter left Tuscumbia without anyone having questioned whether or not he was still a slave. The trip back north went smoothly until the time came to switch steamboats at Paducah, Kentucky. Peter boarded the second steamboat without incident, but the moment the captain saw Peter, he ordered the pilot: Set that fellow ashore!

Peter protested that he had papers stating that he was a free black and had a right to go to Cincinnati.

The captain was not interested in any of Peter's papers. Step right off—step right off! was the reply.

The reason for the captain's actions was that on September 18, 1850—during Peter's visit to his family in Alabama—President Millard Fillmore had signed the Fugitive Slave Law. Until then a rather weak law dating from 1793 had provided for the return of runaway slaves. The new law was passed at the insistence of slaveholders angered at losing thousands of slaves over the Underground Railroad. The Fugitive

Slave Law of 1850 required federal marshals and other officials to assist white persons pursuing fugitives into other states. Anyone who hid or aided a fugitive slave could be jailed for six months and fined $2,000. The steamboat captain simply did not want to have anything to do with a lone black traveler for fear that he would be held responsible if Peter turned out to be an escaped slave.

Peter had to wait an entire day for a vessel to come along whose captain would take him farther up the Ohio River. Then a similar problem arose at Louisville, Kentucky, where he had to switch boats once more. Fortunately two white men from Tuscumbia were at the Louisville wharf and assured the captain that Peter was a loyal slave headed to Cincinnati to rejoin his master. Upon his arrival in Cincinnati, Peter went to visit Isaac Friedman, but found that he had moved to Illinois. Peter then hastened on to Pittsburgh and from there took the stagecoach and train to Philadelphia. Late on the night of November 30, he arrived at his brother William's home.

Peter eagerly described his ten weeks in Alabama for William and Letitia. Then he broached the big question. It would cost perhaps $3,000 to buy his wife and three children out of slavery. During his visit to Tuscumbia, Peter had earned $60, increasing the savings in his purse to about $100. Could William arrange for Peter to borrow the rest of the money so that he could buy his family?

Peter was crushed by his brother's response.

The situation had changed since he had last seen

Peter, William explained. The North and the South had been heading toward war over slavery yet again. To prevent this, Senators Henry Clay of Kentucky, Daniel Webster of Massachusetts, and Stephen Douglas of Illinois had worked out the Compromise of 1850. As part of this deal, California had been allowed to enter the Union on September 9 with no slavery. Congress appeased southern whites by passing the Fugitive Slave Law, which made it unsafe for runaway slaves anywhere on U.S. soil. Peace had been bought at a high price.

The UGRR was busier than ever as a result of the new legislation, only now growing numbers of fugitives were being conducted to Canada, which had outlawed slavery. Many escaped slaves who had lived in Philadelphia for years were packing their belongings and heading north to Canada. UGRR work had also become more dangerous than before. William risked spending six months in jail for each slave he aided—and he sometimes helped fifteen slaves a week!

In the midst of this crisis, William could not obtain the huge sum of $3,000 to free Peter's family. Besides, as a Pennsylvania Anti-Slavery Society official, how could he buy his brother's family while ignoring more than three million other slaves in the United States? Furthermore, the society opposed buying slaves for any reason because it did not recognize the right to own slaves.

"We are anxious," said William, "to help your loved ones escape from bondage. But we cannot bear to give gold to him who has enslaved them." Peter's heart sank, for all these reasons amounted to an answer of no.

But Peter must not despair, William informed him, because there was another way to free his family. A white man who had read William's letter in the August 22 *Pennsylvania Freeman* had offered to go to Alabama to rescue Peter's family. His name was Seth Concklin, and all he asked was $100 for his expenses. The Anti-Slavery Society mainly helped fugitives passing through the Philadelphia area, William explained. Rarely did it send people to rescue slaves and never had it sent a rescuer as far south as Alabama. A few weeks earlier he hadn't thought it possible, William admitted, but Seth had convinced him to give it a try.

Upon first meeting Seth Concklin, Peter was doubtful about the scheme. Concklin certainly didn't *look* like a slave rescuer. Nearly fifty years old, Seth was a small man who refused to carry a gun. But as Peter spoke to Seth and learned about him from others, his hopes soared. Concklin had helped numerous slaves escape over the UGRR in his native New York and later in Illinois. Once in Rochester, New York, he had dashed into a crowd that was about to hang a black man, knocked down the ringleader, and rescued the victim. He had been known to walk fifty miles in a day and row a boat night and day with little pause for food or rest. Although Concklin had been a soldier and was a fine marksman, he refused to carry a gun for fear that the unarmed fugitive slaves might be killed if shooting broke out. Seth preferred the runaways to be captured than shot, which were Peter's feelings exactly.

If his mission succeeded, Concklin said, the rescue of Peter's family would become infamous among

$100 REWARD!

RANAWAY

From the undersigned, living on Current River, about twelve miles above Doniphan, in Ripley County, Mo., on 2nd of March, 1860, A NE GRO MAN, about 30 years old, weighs about 160 pounds; high forehead, with a scar on it; had on brown pants and coat very much worn, and an old black wool hat; shoes size No. 11.

The above reward will be given to any person who may apprehend this said negro out. of the State; and fifty dollars if apprehended in this State outside of Ripley county, or $25 if taken in Ripley county.

APOS TUCKER.

Poster offering a reward for the capture of a runaway slave

slaveholders. They would have to settle in Canada, for they wouldn't be safe anywhere in the United States. Seth told Peter to be ready to meet his family at Windsor, Canada, just across the border from Detroit, Michigan, on about April 1, 1851.

Seth Concklin set out alone from Philadelphia in early January of 1851. In his head he carried directions to the McKiernan plantation, while in his pocket was Vina's cape. Following much the same route Peter had taken, Seth landed in northwest Alabama on the cold, rainy afternoon of Tuesday, January 28, and headed toward the McKiernan plantation. As he walked through the mud, he removed his shoes and rolled his pants up to his knees, for he wanted people to think that he was a poor white man wandering about seeking work.

Through another slave, Seth sent Vina word that a friend wanted to speak to her out in the field that night.

Hoping the "friend" was a rescuer sent by Peter, Vina peeked out her door. She saw no sign of danger, so she slipped out of her cabin and went to the field.

A small, middle-aged man was awaiting her. "Is your name Vina?" he asked.

"Yes, sir," she whispered.

"Are you Peter Friedman's wife?" he asked, knowing she might be confused by the name *Peter Still*.

"Yes, sir, I am his wife," she answered.

"How would you like to go to him?" the stranger offered.

"I'd like it most well, sir, if I could get there," said Vina.

"Well, I have come to take you to him. Can you see me, so as to know me if you should meet me again?"

"No, sir, it's so dark," said Vina. "I can't see your face good."

The stranger held his hand up near Vina's eyes. "If you see me again, you will know me by this hand. You see that half the forefinger is cut off? Do you believe that I came from Peter?"

"I don't know, sir," she answered honestly, worried that she might be falling into some kind of trap.

Seth Concklin pulled the cotton cape Vina had given Peter from his pocket. Vina examined it and saw that it had a hole in one corner. Now she knew that this white stranger had been sent by her husband to rescue her and the children.

"When do you want us to go?" Vina asked.

"I want first to see the boys. Where are they?"

"They're off on the island," Vina said, referring to a nearby island that Mr. McKiernan owned in the

Tennessee River. "They'll come home next Saturday night."

"Well, tell them to come down to the landing Sunday at sunup," said Seth. "I will be there walking about, and if I see two young men, I will keep this hand in sight. Describe it to them, that they will know me. Now, good-bye. Don't be afraid. I will do all I can for you, but you must help yourselves."

Vina returned to her cabin, her heart filled with hope. Peter had done what he had said, and soon the white man with the missing finger would take them to him.

Five days later, on Sunday, February 2, Peter Jr. and Levin met the stranger near the landing at dawn. Seth looked very sleepy, for he had walked about the landing all night so as not to miss the appointment. He held up his hand with the missing finger.

Peter Jr. and Levin accompanied Seth into the woods. The three of them sat on a log, where Seth related his plan and asked for their suggestions. His preparations would require a few weeks, said Seth. Peter Jr., Levin, Catharine, and their mother should come to the landing in the middle of the night of March 1–2, which was a Saturday night into Sunday morning. Knowing that slaves were not allowed calendars but kept track of time by counting Saturdays and Sundays, Seth repeated that they should come to the landing, ready to flee, on the fourth Saturday night from then. He would be there with a little boat, he promised. Then they parted.

By the next day Seth Concklin had crossed the Alabama border to Eastport, Mississippi. There he wrote a letter to William Still, asking him to tell Peter that everything was going well and that the rescue would begin "the first Sunday in March."

Concklin spent the next several weeks scouting the countryside as far north as Indiana and Ohio for the safest route to the North. The Fugitive Slave Law had made people more secretive about helping runaway slaves, but in southern Indiana Seth located several UGRR workers, including a black farmer named Charles Grier and a white man named David Stormont, who would help him. If Seth could take Peter Still's family as far as the Princeton, Indiana, region, Stormont and perhaps a few other UGRR conductors would lead them up Indiana and across lower Michigan to Canada.

Before returning to Alabama, Seth rid himself of the shabby pants and shirt he had been wearing and purchased a respectable suit. He adopted a false identity—a southern slave owner named John H. Miller—and bought a rowboat in Cincinnati, Ohio. For most of the eight-hundred-mile trip back to Alabama, he traveled on steamboats with his rowboat stored aboard the large vessels. Part of the way he paddled along the rivers by himself, probably traveling mostly at night. He timed his long journey so as to arrive at the landing near the McKiernan plantation around the end of February.

Vina and her three children could not get away at the appointed time. Possibly Peter Jr. and Levin were working on Mr. McKiernan's island and could not slip away. In the middle of the night of March 1-2, Seth was waiting at the landing when he received a message: Vina and her children weren't coming, but believed they could meet him in exactly two weeks.

Seth passed the time making more scouting trips. Meanwhile Mr. McKiernan went away on a visit to New Orleans, Louisiana. Claiming that they wanted to buy coffee and sugar for their mother at a store, Peter Jr. and Levin convinced the overseer to grant them passes allowing them to be away from home Saturday night and Sunday, March 15–16. Vina and Catharine obtained passes under the pretext of visiting a friend that same weekend. On Saturday Peter Still's family packed a few belongings. At about midnight they walked from their cabin to the boat landing two miles away.

It was a clear night, and the stars were twinkling. They spied a rowboat by the riverbank, but when Levin whistled, there was no answer. Up and down the river they walked, searching for Seth Concklin. Finally they returned to the rowboat and looked inside. There was Seth, his eyes closed. Exhausted from rowing hundreds of miles, he had fallen asleep while waiting for them.

Seth awoke, and at about three o'clock in the morning, he and the four slaves began their trip along the Tennessee River. With Seth and the boys rowing steadily, at daybreak they reached Eastport, Mississippi, about forty miles into their journey. They had just passed Eastport when they saw a steamboat bearing down on them. Seth told the four fugitives to hide under the blankets, and he paddled the boat to the far side of an island, out of sight of the people on the steamboat. It was fortunate that he did this, for the passengers on the passing vessel included Mr. McKiernan, returning from New Orleans.

To make up some of the fourteen days they had lost by their delayed departure, Seth decided that they should row both day and night. He handled the oars at night, and Peter Jr. and Levin took over during the daytime. Whenever the boys saw another vessel approaching, they called out so that Seth would be in view. That way Seth appeared to be a gentleman being rowed along by his two male slaves. The presence of a woman and a thirteen-year-old girl might raise suspicions, so Vina and Catharine hid beneath the blankets during most of the daylight hours.

Late Monday afternoon there were no other boats in sight, so Seth lay down to rest. He had just fallen asleep when Peter Jr. and Levin yelled out that a boat containing two white men was rapidly approaching from shore.

The strangers demanded to know if there was a white man aboard, suspecting that the two young black

Slaves sometimes attempted to escape by boat.

men were runaway slaves. Seth threw off his blanket and rose to his knees. Seeing the white man, the strangers bowed. They politely asked Seth a few questions.

His name was John H. Miller, answered Seth, and he was headed with his slaves to Paducah, Kentucky, from Eastport, Mississippi. The men bowed again and rowed away. Another time a group of men spotted the black family aboard the boat and ordered Seth Concklin to stop. When Seth ignored them, the men fired their guns at the little vessel. Fortunately the bullets didn't hit anyone. Seth rowed away at full speed, and soon he and his passengers were out of gunshot range.

On Monday a sudden storm struck. Powerful winds nearly dashed the boat against the trees along shore, but Seth managed to guide the vessel to shelter, where they waited an hour while the storm passed.

At dawn, Tuesday, they arrived at Paducah and started up the Ohio River. They followed the river to the Illinois-Indiana border and then headed up the Wabash River. At ten o'clock Sunday morning, March 23, they landed at New Harmony, Indiana, near the state's southwest corner. For the first time in their lives, Vina, Peter Jr., Levin, and Catharine stepped onto free soil.

The four fugitives were ready to celebrate, for now all that remained was to cross the Free States of Indiana and Michigan into Canada. But, warned Concklin, they were in nearly as much danger in the Free States as they had been in the slave states. By this time Mr. McKiernan had probably telegraphed messages around the country offering a reward for his missing slaves. There were "wolves," as Seth called slave catchers, who would gladly seize them for the reward money. Therefore, they must do their walking mainly at night and be extremely cautious.

The first UGRR station they stopped at in Indiana may have been the home of Charles Grier, the black farmer who lived near New Harmony. There, or at another UGRR station, the four fugitives discarded their slave clothes and put on nicer clothing such as free black people might wear.

Following the North Star, Seth led the fugitives through woods and along dirt roads, covering about fifteen miles per night. Something went wrong around Princeton, Indiana. They discovered that David Stormont could not conduct the fugitives onward—perhaps because the two-week delay in departing Alabama had caused them to reach his house much later than expected. Seth Concklin would have to take the fugitives to Canada himself. Although he couldn't get them there by April 1—the date they were to meet Peter—Seth was determined to reach the Canadian border as soon as possible.

On Wednesday or Thursday night, the travelers passed near Vincennes, Indiana. Friday, March 28, was rainy. The roads seemed to be deserted, so Seth thought they could continue walking by day. Vina objected, saying she had a feeling something bad would happen if they traveled by daylight. "If I was you, sir, I'd put off this here jaunt till night," she told Seth, but he ignored his own advice about being cautious and continued to lead them along the muddy roads.

By late afternoon they were on a dirt road about

twenty miles north of Vincennes, Indiana. They were passing a pasture when suddenly a spotted horse galloped up the road. "Stop him!" called a man. Vina quietly told the boys to keep walking and ignore the horse, but Peter Jr., wanting to help, caught the animal and led him back to his owner.

A little farther along they passed a large white man standing outside a sawmill. Studying the little group, he asked Vina, "How de do, Aunt Lucy, which way are you traveling?" Her heart pounding, Vina pretended that she hadn't heard him.

Before night they approached their next refuge, the home of a Quaker, about twenty-five miles north of Vincennes. Seth pointed the fugitives to a smaller house where the Quaker's son lived. Seth thought they would be safe there while he went to the main house to inform the stationmaster of their arrival.

Vina and her children were admitted to the small house. While warming themselves by the fire, they suddenly heard the pounding of horses' hooves. They looked through the window and counted seven men tying their horses to the fence. One was the man with the spotted horse that Peter Jr. had captured for him that afternoon, and another was the fellow who had tauntingly called Vina *Aunt Lucy*.

"They come after us!" whispered one of Vina's sons.

"Yes," said their mother, "I'll lay anything we're gonna be took now!"

The men had tracked the fugitives' footprints in the mud. Within a few seconds three or four of them had blocked the doors while the others burst into the house and began questioning Vina and her children. All of the men had knives and pistols in their belts.

"Where are you headed?" the leader demanded of Peter Jr.

"To Springfield, Illinois, sir," he answered, as Seth Concklin had instructed him to say in such an emergency.

"Do you belong to the man that brought you here?"

"Yes, sir."

"Where did you come from?"

"From Kentucky, sir," said Peter Jr. "Master died last year, and now his brother's taking us on to his farm."

"I'll be damned if I don't believe he stole you all!" said the leader.

The seven men huddled together, deciding what to do. Peter Jr. and Levin wanted to fight, but they were unarmed and outnumbered. In a while one of the men went out, returning shortly with a wagon and a jug of liquor. After drinking heartily, the men tied the brothers' hands behind their backs. The boys were marched outside with their mother and sister, both of whom remained untied.

Vina and her three children were shoved into the back of the wagon. Two or three of the slave catchers sat up front in the vehicle while the others rode alongside as guards. They had just started out when Seth Concklin, having observed what had occurred from the Quaker's house, came running after them and leaped into the wagon. Seth began untying the captives but was quickly seized by the guards on horseback.

"Stop or I'll blow your brains out!" one of the men threatened.

Seth obeyed the command and was allowed to

remain in the wagon. The slave catchers drove the fugitives twenty-five miles south to the jail in Vincennes and told the jailer that the black people were undoubtedly escaped slaves. Seth could not produce papers proving that he owned them, nor could Vina and her family prove that they were free blacks. The jailer seemed to feel sorry for the black family. However, he was afraid to violate the Fugitive Slave Law, so he locked them up, at the same time telling Seth Concklin he was free to go.

Concklin remained in Vincennes. He visited the fugitives every day, reassuring them through the jailhouse window that he would think of a way to free them. Vina warned him to flee before he was locked up, too. But Seth felt responsible for this disaster and refused to abandon them.

Peter's family had been in the Vincennes jail a short time when officials in the town received a telegraph message:

Four likely negroes have been stolen from Bernard McKiernan, near South Florence, Alabama. Their owner has offered a reward of four hundred dollars for them, and six hundred for the apprehension of the thief, and his delivery to South Florence.

McKiernan had offered $200 more for Concklin's arrest than he had for the return of his slaves. The next time Seth visited the jail, he was arrested.

Telegraph messages were exchanged between Alabama and Indiana. Convinced that the captured fugitives belonged to him, McKiernan headed to the North to retrieve them. One night around the time that Peter had expected to meet his family in Canada, Catharine and her brothers were sleeping in their jail cell while Vina lay awake worrying about what would become of them. Suddenly Vina's thoughts were interrupted by a familiar voice outside their cell:

"I wish you would let me in. I would like to see them."

The key turned in the lock and the jailer, holding a lantern, entered the cell with Mr. McKiernan and another man. McKiernan approached the bed on which the four slaves were lying and looked down at them in disgust. "Boy, what are you doing here?" demanded McKiernan, pointing his cane at Peter Jr. "Speak, you rascal, or I'll knock you in the head with this stick!"

"Don't know, sir," Peter Jr. said quietly.

"*Don't know!'* I'll make you tell a different tale when I get you home. You, Levin, don't you think this is a devil of a caper?"

Levin was silent, so McKiernan turned to Vina. "See here, girl, how came you to leave home?"

When Vina didn't answer, McKiernan said, "Ain't it damned astonishing you all can't answer when you're spoken to? That rascal Peter is at the bottom of this," he told his companion. "He got in with a Jew and persuaded him to buy him. If Peter and that Jew ever show their heads in Tuscumbia again, I'll have them hung sky-high!"

They had better start talking, McKiernan warned. The fugitives protected Seth Concklin by telling a story they had rehearsed. Four strangers had stolen them from the McKiernan plantation. Only later, while being carried away by the strangers, had they met Mr. Miller.

McKiernan then went to the next cell, where Concklin was being held. Seth refused to reveal any information. "It's damned astonishing that you won't tell who started you in this business," said McKiernan. "Would you be such a fool as to be carried back in irons and lose your life for the sake of saving other people?"

"It is of no use for you to question me about them," answered Concklin. "You have me now, and it is not worthwhile to bring other people into trouble."

Early the next morning, Mr. McKiernan returned. The five prisoners were taken from jail—Vina's sons and Seth Concklin in chains—and placed in a coach with McKiernan and the man he had brought along as a guard. The coach carried them to Evansville, Indiana, not far from where they had landed at New Harmony on a happier day about a week earlier. At Evansville they boarded a steamboat called the *Paul Anderson* and started for Alabama down the Ohio River.

Near Paducah, Kentucky, Seth Concklin vanished from the steamboat, perhaps while Mr. McKiernan was guarding him alone. McKiernan informed Peter Still's family by merely saying, "Well, that rascal's gone."

Concklin's body soon washed up on the Ohio River shore. How he died remains a mystery to this day. Knowing he would receive a severe punishment in Alabama, Concklin had tried to escape but had drowned, asserted proslavery people. Abolitionists insisted that Seth wouldn't have jumped off a boat with his hands and feet in chains. They claimed that when Seth's body was found his skull was fractured, indicating that he had been hit on the head and pushed overboard—most likely by McKiernan. Seth Concklin was buried by the banks of the Ohio River near where he was found, his body still in chains.

A few days later Vina, Peter Jr., Levin, and Catharine were returned to the McKiernan plantation.

As soon as Seth Concklin left Philadelphia to rescue his family, Peter had moved to his mother's house in New Jersey. He did odd jobs for neighboring farmers, earning a little money, but mostly he waited. On March 24 Concklin sent a letter to William Still at the Anti-Slavery Society Office saying that Peter's family had just arrived in the Free State of Indiana and they expected to be in Canada in several weeks. Peter then went to stay with his sister Mary in Philadelphia so that he could quickly depart when he received word that his family had arrived in Canada. Each day he looked forward to receiving a telegram or letter telling him where to meet Vina and his children.

One day around April 10, Peter entered the parlor of Mary's house and found her sitting and reading a newspaper. Peter immediately knew something was wrong because she had tears in her eyes.

Mary showed him the paper and asked if he had heard the news.

Peter told her that he couldn't read, so his sister then read aloud from the *Philadelphia Public Ledger*:

RUNAWAY NEGROES CAUGHT

At Vincennes, Indiana, on Saturday last, a white man and four negroes were arrested. The negroes belong to B. McKiernan of South Florence, Alabama, and the man who was running them off calls himself John H. Miller. The prisoners were taken charge of by the Marshall of Evansville.

Peter Still was devastated. His family had been returned to McKiernan's plantation, perhaps to be sold; and as he would soon learn, Seth Concklin was dead.

For a long time Peter felt deeply discouraged, convinced that he was doomed to never see his loved ones again. One day, when they were together, his brother William tried to console Peter.

"You ought not to feel so uneasy—so perfectly restless because your family are slaves," said William. "There are thousands of people as good as they who are in the same condition. Do you see that woman across the street?" he asked, pointing out the window of the Anti-Slavery Society Office. "She is just as good as you are, and she has a mother and sisters in slavery."

Suddenly Peter felt that William didn't understand, and that he never *could* understand because he had never been a slave. "Look here," Peter said angrily to his brother, "I know a heap of men as good as I am and as smart as I am that are slaves now. But I've bought my liberty, and my family shall be free!"

He parted from his brother feeling renewed hope that he would find a way to free his wife and children.

Slave father being separated from his family, from The Child's
Anti-Slavery Book, *published in 1860*

CHAPTER XIV

"Peter's Sent for You All!"

Mr. McKiernan returned Vina and her children to his plantation on Saturday, April 5, 1851. They were immediately sent out to plant cotton. For four days nothing was done about their escape attempt. Then on Wednesday Mr. McKiernan and the overseer approached Vina and Peter Jr. in the cotton field. First Peter Jr. was ordered to remove his shirt. The overseer gave him two hundred lashes, while McKiernan sat on his horse and watched.

When the whipping ended, Peter Jr., his back dripping blood, defiantly cried to the overseer, "This is the last time that you shall strike me! I never will be whipped again by any man!"

"Hush your mouth, you damned rascal," Mr. McKiernan warned him, "or I'll have two hundred more stripes put on you!"

McKiernan and the overseer left Peter Jr. lying on the ground and turned to Vina. She received about one hundred lashes, which was considered a light punishment for running away.

Next McKiernan and the overseer went to the plantation's blacksmith shop, where Levin was at work. Two hundred strokes of the whip left his back bruised and bloody.

McKiernan questioned Catharine, but she seemed to know so little about the escape that he did not have her whipped. "It's that devilish Peter and the Jew that are at the bottom of all this," McKiernan said to the overseer in front of Catharine. "It would be just like Vina to try it again, but she'll never run away and leave her daughter. So it's best to keep one of them on the island—I reckon the old woman."

By "old woman" McKiernan meant Vina, who was about forty years old at this time. The following Sunday Vina was rowed out to the island to join the small group of McKiernan's slaves who grew cotton there. On the island Vina lived in a little hut.

McKiernan found another way to discourage Peter Still's family from running away. Each August McKiernan gathered his slaves for a barbecue. During the festivities he made certain that one or two couples were married, because slave marriages meant more slave babies. At the barbecue in August of 1851, McKiernan asked Peter Jr. if he would like to marry a girl named Susanna.

Only his promise to his father that he would remain single had prevented Peter Jr. from marrying Susanna already, for, as everyone on the plantation knew, the two of them had loved each other since childhood. But Peter Jr. said that he didn't want to marry. He believed that his father would yet rescue them and that his promise was still in force.

"But Susanna says she loves you, and you ought to have her," insisted Mr. McKiernan, thinking that escape for the family would be much more difficult if Peter Jr. had a wife and child.

"No, sir, I don't care about marrying without my mother's willing," Peter Jr. replied.

"It's no matter about your *mother*, boy!" McKiernan angrily told the twenty-four-year-old slave. "*I* give you leave. Go and dress yourself to get married and then come back to me!"

As he changed clothes, Peter was filled with contrary feelings. In his heart he wanted to marry Susanna, yet in obeying his owner, he disobeyed his father.

Dressed in her best clothes, Susanna met Peter Jr. in the yard where McKiernan had ordered them to appear. A fellow slave said a few words to marry them.

"Why don't you march with the others?" McKiernan asked Vina and her son Levin, both of whom had watched the marriage "ceremony" silently while cooking food for the barbecue.

"I ain't a soldier," Vina replied sullenly, "and I don't know nothing about marching."

"Better mind how you talk, girl—or I'll give you a slap!" her owner threatened.

Peter Jr. moved into the cabin where his wife, Susanna, lived with her mother, "Aunt" Patsey. In about a year Susanna gave birth to a boy she and Peter Jr. named Edmund. Despite her initial anger over the forced marriage, Vina loved Susanna and adored her grandchild.

That winter, when Edmund was just a few months old, he came down with whooping cough. Pneumonia set in, and Edmund became gravely ill. Susanna asked to stay at home for a few days to nurse her baby, but the overseer refused. Desperate, Susanna turned to Mrs. McKiernan, hoping a woman would understand. But Mrs. McKiernan ordered her to the fields. A week later little Edmund died.

In March of 1854 Susanna gave birth to another son. The child was named Peter in honor of his father and grandfather. When baby Peter was five weeks old, Mr. McKiernan ordered Susanna out to help prepare for planting, even though she was still weak following childbirth. A heavy rain fell soon after Susanna returned to the field, and she became ill—with what malady is not known.

Susanna worked another week, but by then she was so ill she couldn't go out anymore. A doctor was called in to no avail. Month after month Susanna grew weaker. On a Sunday morning in August she told her husband, "I'm going away from you now, Peter, but I shall leave our baby with you. You'll take good care of him for my sake, won't you?" After the sun went down, Susanna died, at about twenty-five years of age.

Vina, meanwhile, was on the island most of the time. Occasionally Catharine or one of her sons joined her there, but McKiernan was careful to keep the family apart.

One winter day, when Vina and Catharine were on the island together, McKiernan rowed over for a visit. He found Vina and her daughter clearing the field of "trash," as debris from the cotton plants was called, and burning it so that the ground would be ready for the spring plowing.

McKiernan sat down by the fire and called Vina to him.

From the look on his face by the glowing firelight, Vina knew what he wanted. Now about sixty years old, McKiernan had been trying to rape her or talk her into having sex with him for more than twenty years. She ignored him, continuing to throw the trash from the field into the fire.

McKiernan told her he intended to stay the night on the island and asked her to spend the night with him.

Vina couldn't ignore him any longer. "What you mean, sir, by asking me such a thing as that?" she said. "I haven't forgot how you've abused me and my children."

"If you will come to my house, I'll do all I can for you, and you shall never want for anything," he promised.

"No, sir, I never will come to your house," said Vina. "There's a little old hut yonder, what don't keep the rain out nights. I can stay there like I have done. Now, wouldn't it be mighty strange if I didn't hate you, knowing so much about your ways as I do? I tell you, sir, I never did like you, and I never shall!"

"The devil!" shouted McKiernan. "Don't you stand there and tell me you don't like me!"

But Vina was angrier than he was. "Well, sir, I don't like you, and I'll never put myself in your power while I live."

"What's that girl's name of yours there?" demanded McKiernan.

"You know her name, sir, just as well as I do. Her

name Catharine. Why, what you gonna say about her?"

"I say she's a devilish likely girl—" he began.

"Now, Master," warned Vina, "I want to tell you, if you ever come a-fooling round her, you'll be sorry. I'd rather die a peaceable death than be hung, but just as sure as you meddle with my daughter, I'll do what I say. I'll kill you."

Vina knew that she risked being beaten or tortured to death for threatening her master, but Mr. McKiernan walked away and never tormented her again. At the time she believed it was because she had scared him or even touched his conscience. Perhaps there was a bit of truth to that, but McKiernan backed off for another reason that Vina wouldn't know about for two or three years.

When he learned of his family's capture and Seth Concklin's death, Peter Still didn't know what to do. Gradually he realized that all was not lost. A brave man had died trying to rescue his family, but because Seth had not carried a gun, there had been no shooting. At least Vina, Peter Jr., Levin, and Catharine were alive.

Thinking more clearly as his spirits rose, Peter realized that another rescue attempt was out of the question. McKiernan would be watching Vina and the children too carefully for that. Only one possibility remained. Peter had to return to his original plan of buying his family's freedom.

First he had to know how much it would cost to free his wife and children. Mrs. McKiernan had mentioned $3,000—an enormous amount—but that was just talk. The true sum could be more or less. Peter

asked several abolitionist friends, including Samuel
Lewis of Cincinnati, to write letters asking McKiernan's
price for Vina and their sons and daughter. Peter's
friends did so, requesting that McKiernan direct his
answer to William Still of Philadelphia.

A few days later McKiernan responded, making his
points clear even though he had difficulty spelling
many words, including his own name:

SOUTH FLORENCE ALA
6 Augest 1851

Mr. WILLIAM STILL
North Fifth street Philadelphia

> *Sir a few days sinc [I received] a letter . . . in*
> *behalf of a Negro man by the name of peter . . .*
> *the object of the letter was to purchis from me 4*
> *Negros that is peters wife & 3 children 2 sons & 1*
> *Girl the Name of said Negres are the woman*
> *Viney (the mother), Eldest son peter, second son*
> *Leven, 1 Girl about 13 or 14 years old. The*
> *Husband & Father . . . was sold to a man by the*
> *Name of Freeman who removed to cincinnati*
> *ohio & Tuck peter with him of course peter*
> *became free. . . . Last march a white man by*
> *the name of Miller abducted the bove negroes*
> *was caut at vincanes Indi with said negroes . . .*
> *& on his return met his Just reward by Getting*
> *drownded. . . . I recovered & Braught Back said*
> *4 negroes under the Belief that peter the Husband*
> *was accessery to the offence thareby putting me*

*to much Expense & Truble to the amt $1000
which if he gets them he must refund. These 4
negroes are worth in the market about 4000
for they are Extraordinary fine. . . . You can
say to Peter & his new discovered Relations in
philadelphia I will take 5000 for the 4 culerd
people & if he can raise the money I will delever
said negroes. Say to peter to let me Know his
viewes amediately as I am determined to act in a
way if he dont take this offer he will never have
an other oppertunity*

B. McKIERNON

As his brother William finished reading the letter
aloud, Peter was jolted by the final words: *Say to Peter
if he don't take this offer he will never have another
opportunity.* McKiernan was threatening to sell Peter's
family if he didn't receive the $5,000 soon.

Raising that much money was impossible, William
sadly told Peter. His own salary was small, and the
rest of the Still family combined couldn't scrape
together $5,000 (which would equal about $100,000
in today's money). Furthermore, not only did the
Anti-Slavery Society oppose buying slaves, the organization's meager resources were under great strain
at this time. Since the passage of the Fugitive Slave
Law, a number of black people in the Philadelphia
area had been reclaimed as slaves and taken to the
South. Besides sheltering fugitives and sending them
on to Canada, the society had become involved in
several legal battles.

One noteworthy case involved Euphemia Williams. After living in Philadelphia as a free person for more than twenty years, she was arrested under the Fugitive Slave Law in February of 1851 and imprisoned. A Maryland planter asserted that she had fled from him twenty-two years earlier and must be returned. Although Euphemia's six children had all been born in Pennsylvania, the planter claimed that he owned them, too, because their mother had escaped from him. The only way to prevent the family from being dragged off as slaves was to show that Euphemia Williams wasn't the person who had escaped from Maryland. James Miller McKim and William Still helped find witnesses who testified that Euphemia Williams had never been a slave. The judge ruled in Williams's favor, allowing her and her children to remain free.

Also in the early 1850s, slave hunters kidnapped Rachel and Elizabeth Parker, two black sisters from Chester County, Pennsylvania, outside Philadelphia. They claimed that the girls were fugitive slaves. A group of abolitionists including Joseph C. Miller chased the kidnappers all the way to Maryland. But the kidnappers captured and murdered Miller, jailed Rachel Parker in Maryland, and sold her sister Elizabeth down to Louisiana. The Pennsylvania Anti-Slavery Society helped wage a legal battle that freed the girls and returned them to their mother in Chester County. Miller's murderers were not apprehended, however.

William couldn't supply Peter with $5,000, but he aided his brother in other ways. He helped him obtain a job as a servant and carriage driver for Mrs.

Mary Buckman of Burlington, New Jersey. Mrs. Buckman and her two daughters not only employed Peter, they taught him to read and write. But Peter figured that even if he could save half his weekly $5 salary, it would take him forty years to accumulate $5,000.

William had another idea. Perhaps an appeal to Mr. McKiernan's conscience would convince him to lower his price for Peter's family or even prompt him to set them free without charge. A few days after receiving McKiernan's letter, William Still wrote back to him:

PHILADELPHIA, Aug. 16th, 1851

To B. McKIERNAN, ESQ.:

Sir—

I have received your letter under date of the 6th. . . . As regards the price fixed upon by you for the family, I must say I do not think it possible to raise half that amount, though Peter authorized me to say he would give you twenty-five hundred for them. Probably he is not as well aware as I am, how difficult it is to raise so large a sum of money. . . . I am employed as a clerk for a living, but my salary is quite too limited to enable me to contribute any great amount towards so large a sum as is demanded. We have plenty of friends, but little money. Now, sir, allow me to make an appeal to your humanity. . . . Would your heart or your conscience [allow you to] restore to them,

*without price, that dear freedom, which is theirs
by right of nature? Would you not feel a
satisfaction in so doing which all the wealth of
the world could not equal? At all events, could
you not so reduce the price as to place it in the
power of Peter's relatives and friends to raise the
means for their purchase? Hoping, sir, to hear
from you,*

WM. STILL

William Still's appeal to McKiernan's "humanity,"
"heart," and "conscience" failed. McKiernan refused to
reduce the price and did not even bother to answer this
letter. Peter's choices were clear: He must raise $4,700
(for by this time he had saved about $300) or he would
never see his family again.

Peter thought of a plan—probably with his brother
William's help. He would travel around the country
telling his story in churches, town halls, and everywhere else people might pay to hear him. He would
talk to abolitionists and businessmen, ministers and
authors, politicians and teachers, and he would knock
on the doors of rich people. He would speak to people
day and night, and he wouldn't stop until he had
$5,000.

The Pennsylvania Anti-Slavery Society helped him
plan out his tour. On November 8, 1852—almost
exactly two years to the day since he had last seen Vina
and their children—Peter set out from his mother's
house in Burlington, New Jersey. Fifty-two years old,
he had the energy of a man of twenty-two, for he now

Pages from Peter Still's Freedom Account

had hope that he could free his family if he raised the money before McKiernan sold them. Around the time that Peter began his fund-raising travels, someone gave him a pocket ledger. Peter called it his *Freedom Account* and used it to record the money he accumulated.

First he visited John Nelson Still, a brother he had never met before, in Brooklyn, New York. A leading black businessman, John Nelson operated a tailor shop, a secondhand clothing store, and a barber supply business. John Nelson donated about $50 to the cause, and told Peter to let him know if there was anything else he could do to help.

From Brooklyn Peter went to Syracuse, New York,

where he met the abolitionist minister Samuel Joseph May, who wrote him letters of introduction to other antislavery leaders around the country. While visiting Syracuse, he was also reunited with Mrs. Kate Pickard, whom he had known at the Tuscumbia Female Seminary in Alabama. The former teacher provided him with more letters of introduction and asked Peter if she could write up his life story in a book.

Peter recalled Euphemia Williams, who had been claimed along with her children as slaves after many years of living in freedom. What if the Saunders Griffin family read about Peter Still's mother, brothers, and sisters? Might they not claim all of them because Peter's mother had run away nearly fifty years earlier? Peter thanked Mrs. Pickard, but said he didn't think a book was a good idea.

From Syracuse Peter continued a short way west to Auburn, New York. There he spoke for the first time before a large audience—at a Reverend Millard's church. When the minister invited him up to the pulpit, Peter was terrified, but once he began speaking, his story poured out of him. He related how he and his brother Levin had been separated from their mother and sisters as children and taken down to Kentucky and later Alabama. He described the beating Levin had suffered for marrying without permission and his brother's early death. Peter talked about his wife, Vina, who also had been separated from her mother, and about their children Peter Jr., Levin, and Catharine as well as those who had died. Peter recounted waiting forty years before he found friends who helped him become free and told how he had saved pennies and dimes until finally purchasing himself at the age of fifty. He informed them about Seth Concklin, a New York man who had died in a valiant attempt to rescue Vina and their children. And he explained that, if he could raise $5,000, his family's freedom was within his grasp. By the time Peter finished, tears were streaming down his face, and for the first time in their lives, slavery had real meaning for many of his listeners.

During his week in Auburn, he spoke at several churches, raising a total of $50. From Auburn, he passed through Waterloo, New York, where he received perhaps $10. He then continued on to Rochester, where he remained for about two weeks, earning another $200 from his speaking engagements.

After Rochester, Peter headed to Massachusetts. In the town of Andover he spoke in a church, earning $40, and also visited author Harriet Beecher Stowe, who had recently published her famous antislavery novel, *Uncle Tom's Cabin.* In the North Stowe was being hailed for revealing the evils of slavery, but in the South her novel was so despised that a person caught reading it risked being sentenced to jail. Stowe listened to Peter's real-life story and was so moved that she wrote the following letter for him:

> *Having examined the claims of this unfortunate man, I am satisfied that his is a case that calls for compassion and aid.*
>
> *Though the sum demanded is so large as to look hopeless, yet if every man who is so happy as to be free, and have his own wife and children*

*for his own, would give even twenty-five cents,
the sum might soon be raised.*

*As ye would that men should do for you—do
ye even so for them.*

H. B. Stowe

Peter went to Boston, a leading abolitionist center, around New Year's Day of 1853. For the next three months, he spoke often in Boston and in neighboring towns, raising $460. Then he headed north from Massachusetts to Maine, where he received $100 in Portland. Over the next few weeks, he collected an additional $390 during visits to Brunswick, Bath, Saco, and Biddeford in Maine; Portsmouth and Hampton in New Hampshire; and Newburyport back in Massachusetts.

In June of 1853 he returned to Burlington, New Jersey, for a brief rest. Over the past seven months, he had visited more than twenty towns, accumulating about $1,400. While Peter rested, his mother, brother William, and other relatives in New Jersey and Philadelphia scraped together more than $50 for him. Counting the $300 in savings with which he had started, and subtracting his traveling expenses, Peter now had a total of about $1,600. When William questioned whether he could collect the entire $5,000, Peter assured his brother, "The Lord won't let me fail," and set out once again.

Peter spent the Fourth of July in Brooklyn with his brother John Nelson, who contributed another $50 or so. From there he returned to Syracuse, collecting

$125 in a few days. Not far from Syracuse in Peterboro, New York, he visited with Gerrit Smith, a wealthy politician who had devoted much of his fortune to such causes as helping slaves escape to Canada, women's rights, and assisting the poor. Smith gave him a sizable donation.

Peter Still lived in dread of one thing: What if McKiernan sold his family before he accumulated the $5,000? Realizing that time was against him, he quickened his pace. He hurried from town to town in Massachusetts: Boston . . . New Bedford . . . Fall River . . . Lowell . . . Somerville . . . Cambridge . . . Worcester . . . Plymouth. By the end of October of 1853 he had over $2,500—more than half the required sum.

He spent November of 1853 in Providence, Rhode Island, where he spoke at several churches, recording $250 in his Freedom Account. In early 1854 Peter visited New York City, quickly amassing $1,146, probably with his brother John Henry's aid. By this time newspaper articles had been written about his quest to free his wife and children, and even in the South "Peter Still's case" was known. Down in Alabama Bernard McKiernan was surprised and pleased, for he had set a high price thinking that there was little possibility of Peter actually paying it. When McKiernan let Vina get away with threatening to kill him, it was probably because he realized that she and her children would soon bring him $5,000.

Spring 1854 found Peter in Albany, the capital of New York, where he collected $75. From there he went on to the Massachusetts cities of Pittsfield and

Springfield, where he obtained $105 and $100 respectively. By June of 1854 Peter had more than $4,000, but another problem arose. There would be transportation costs for bringing his family to the North, so he needed a lot more money than he had anticipated.

In the summer of 1854 he visited Connecticut's twin capitals, New Haven and Hartford, receiving $300 in each city. He proceeded through Connecticut, obtaining $21 in Wethersfield, $126 in Middletown, $80 in Meriden, $136 in Bridgeport, $115 in New London, and $100 in Norwich.

Peter Still now had more than $5,000.

He asked friends to write to Mr. McKiernan informing him that the money was ready. While awaiting an answer, Peter spoke a few more times. He received $45 in Northampton, Massachusetts, and $80 in Buffalo, New York, for telling his story. From Buffalo he crossed into Canada—perhaps to evaluate the possibility of moving his family there. He spoke to the congregations of two black churches in Toronto, collecting $15.

His final visit was to the village of Camillus, New York, where he spoke at two churches on Sunday, October 22, 1854. The minister at one of the churches told his flock: "Peter can succeed without our aid. But we cannot afford to lose this opportunity [to help humanity]." Peter left Camillus with another $63.

Peter Still returned to Philadelphia with about $5,500 and waited. He was near collapse from two years of traveling around the country and from constant worry. What if, so near his goal, something went wrong? What if his family had been sold or one of them had died? What if Mr. McKiernan suddenly raised the price or decided not to sell them at all?

In late 1854 McKiernan sent Peter a letter. He refused to do business with a black person, said McKiernan. But if Peter sent a white man down to Florence, Alabama, with $5,000, McKiernan would release Peter's family to him.

A friend of William Still's in Philadelphia agreed to serve as Peter's agent. This unidentified young white man placed Peter's $5,000 and the money for the transportation costs in his coat pocket—along with a pistol in case anything went wrong—and headed for the South. On or about December 15, he arrived in Florence, Alabama, where he met Bernard McKiernan's agent, a merchant named John Simpson. Meanwhile Peter set out for Cincinnati, Ohio, to wait for Vina and his children.

On Sunday, December 17, 1854, Vina was sitting alone in her hut on the island when a slave woman stopped by to visit.

"What do you think, Vina?" asked the woman. "I heard a great secret in town last night. Peter's sent for you all! And there's a man in town what come from someplace in the North, to tote you all off."

"How do you know?" asked Vina, trembling with excitement.

"Last night I was in Mr. Simpson's store, and they were making out the papers!"

Vina told her sons, who were with her on the island, what she had heard. But nothing happened until early Wednesday morning, when the slaves on the island were rowed over to the home plantation to help kill hogs.

At ten in the morning, as the slaves were butchering the hogs, Bernard McKiernan approached Vina. "Well, Vina," he said, "how would you like to see Peter? He's bought you all."

"If it's true, sir," she answered, "I'd like to go mighty well."

"If it's true? Don't you suppose I can sell you if I choose? If you want to go, make haste and get yourselves ready. I've got to carry you all over to Florence tonight. There's a man there who has come to you from Peter." McKiernan then informed Peter Jr. and Levin, and sent the overseer to fetch Catharine.

"Give me your ax, girl," the overseer told Catharine, who was chopping down a tree. "Go to the house. You're sold, and your master sent me for you in a hurry."

Fearing that they had been sold to a new owner, Catharine ran to her mother. "What is it, Mother?" she asked.

"Your father's sent for us, child," said Vina, trying to control her excitement in case this turned out to be some kind of a trick.

Something else troubled the family as they packed their belongings. Peter hadn't known about the existence of his grandson, who was nine months old. Vina approached McKiernan to ask if little Peter was included in the sale.

"You would like to take your little grandchild with you?" McKiernan asked, raising her hopes.

"Yes, sir," answered Vina, "if I could."

"I'd sell him to you for a trifle—perhaps a hundred dollars," said McKiernan. Otherwise, the baby would stay behind on the plantation with his other grandmother, Aunt Patsey.

Vina returned to Peter Jr. to tell her son the bad news. Remembering Susanna's dying words—*"You'll take care of him for my sake, won't you?"*—Peter Jr. went to beg McKiernan to include his son.

"The baby?" said McKiernan. "Oh, you may have it for two hundred dollars."

Peter Jr.'s heart sank, for, as their owner knew, they did not have the money.

That evening Vina, Catharine, Peter Jr., and Levin said farewell to their friends on the plantation. They climbed into a wagon with Bernard McKiernan, who was to take them across the river to Florence, where he would sign the final papers with Peter's agent. Baby Peter seems to have been taken along to spend the last hours with his family until they departed for the North.

By the time they reached the river, it was too dark to cross over to Florence, so they spent the night at the home of a friend of McKiernan's. Then they crossed the river early the next morning and went to John Simpson's store to meet with the young Philadelphian.

Up to the last moment, Vina and Peter Jr. begged McKiernan to let them take the baby with them. Their tears moved several white people in John Simpson's store to protest.

"I say, McKiernan," one gentleman said, "I think you ought to give this old woman her grandchild. Give them the little one for good measure."

"Oh, I'll sell the child cheap to them," he replied.

"Sell it? They've no money to buy it," said another man. "Give it to them—that would be no more than fair."

But he wouldn't budge. "Peter's got rich relations and friends in Philadelphia," McKiernan insisted, adding that Peter could send a few hundred dollars later to buy his grandson.

At last the papers were completed. McKiernan took Peter Jr.'s baby from him. Then Vina, Peter Jr., Levin, and Catharine climbed into a coach with Peter's emissary. They traveled to Waterloo, Alabama, where they were to board a northbound steamboat.

The steamboat captain at Waterloo was afraid that Vina and her children were fugitive slaves, and he did not want to allow them onto his vessel. The young white man showed the captain the papers proving that he had purchased the black people, keeping secret the fact that he had bought them on behalf of their husband and father. After much arguing, the captain allowed the young man aboard with his four slaves.

The same thing happened when they tried to change boats at Paducah, Kentucky. Again the young man convinced the captain that Vina and the children were his property.

But when it was time to change boats at Louisville, Kentucky, the captain absolutely refused to let them board. His boat was headed to Cincinnati, which was free soil. If these black people were fugitive slaves, he didn't want to be blamed.

Fortunately the young man knew a merchant in Louisville who could assist them. As they accompanied the young man to see his friend, Vina and her sons and daughter were afraid that they were being taken to be sold, for Louisville was on slave soil. Their fears remained until the merchant secured tickets for them on the next boat for Cincinnati.

Meanwhile Peter had been waiting in Cincinnati since Christmas Eve. Each morning he walked down to the wharf to see if his family was on the steamboat from Louisville. And each morning the passengers poured down the gangplank, but Peter's loved ones were not among them. By December 31 Peter's hopes had turned to fear. As he walked to the wharf on that last morning of 1854, his legs trembled beneath him. What if the young white man his brother William had sent to Alabama had run off with the money and abandoned Peter's family? What if the young man had been killed like Seth Concklin and Peter's family had been kidnapped and sold? There were a thousand things that could go wrong between the McKiernan plantation in Alabama and the free soil of Cincinnati, Ohio.

The morning boat from Louisville arrived. Its name was the *Northerner*, but Peter didn't notice, because four people along the railing were waving at him. He ran aboard the steamboat and, crying with joy, clasped his wife, daughter, and sons to his heart.

Peter Still and his wife and children were together and free at last.

CHAPTER XV

"LONGING TO BE FREE"

Peter and Vina Still and their children remained in Cincinnati for two days. They stayed with Levi and Katie Coffin, a Quaker couple who over a period of thirty-five years helped more than three thousand slaves escape on the UGRR. While in Cincinnati they also visited with relatives of Peter's former owners, Joseph and Isaac Friedman.

On January 3, 1855, Peter Still and his family left Cincinnati. Heading east, they reached Philadelphia on January 10 and arrived at Peter's mother's house in Burlington, New Jersey, soon after. Charity Still, now well into her seventies, greeted Peter's family with a stirring passage from the Bible. "I had not thought to see thy face," she said to her son Peter. Then, turning to Vina, Peter Jr., Levin, and Catharine, she continued, "And, lo, God hath shewed me also thy seed [children]."

What became of little Peter, the nine-month-old child left in slavery? Apparently his grandfather and father, Peter Still and Peter Still Jr., tried to buy him from McKiernan but failed. The baby became very ill soon after his relatives departed Alabama. The Peter Still papers at the Special Collections and University Archives at Rutgers University in New Jersey contain a letter sent on June 25, 1855, to Peter Still (the grandfather) from a friend in Alabama who informed him:

Peter Still

Dear Sir—

> *Respecting your little grand son Peter he was born March 11th 1854 when your family left he was sick & hardly expected to live but he is well now and a very fine child and figuratively speaking is yourself. His head, eyes, mouth, and complexion are a perfect picture of you.*

Even after little Peter recovered, his father could not get him back. Exactly why is unknown. One possibility is that his maternal grandmother, Aunt Patsey, did not want to give him up, even though it meant keeping him in slavery.

Peter Still and his family lived briefly with relatives and friends in the Burlington, New Jersey, area. Then Peter and Vina were hired to work in a Burlington boardinghouse. Their salaries enabled them to purchase a little farm in Burlington near Peter's mother's home. Peter and Vina lived quietly on this ten-acre farm, growing vegetables that they sold in town.

William Still helped his niece and nephews begin their new lives. He assisted Levin in finding work as a blacksmith in Beverly, New Jersey, within walking distance of his parents' and grandmother's homes, and helped Peter Jr. obtain a job, apparently as a house servant and carriage driver, with Richard Ely just across the border in New Hope, Pennsylvania. William and Letitia welcomed Catharine, or *Katie* as they called her, into their home so that she could attend school in Philadelphia. What's more, they paid for her schooling.

Little is recorded about Peter and Vina Still's later years. We know that they were among the eleven organizers of Burlington's Second Baptist Church, the oldest black Baptist church in New Jersey's Burlington County. And we know that Peter and Vina finally allowed the teacher, Kate Pickard, to write a book about them. Mrs. Pickard visited Peter and Vina, who recounted their experiences for her. Published in 1856 in Syracuse, New York, Pickard's book was entitled *The Kidnapped and the Ransomed, Being the Personal Recollections of Peter Still and His Wife "Vina," After Forty Years of Slavery*. Peter honored his dead brother, Levin, with the following dedication:

TO THE MEMORY OF LEVIN STILL; AND OF ALL THE BRAVE-HEARTED MEN AND WOMEN, WHO LIKE HIM HAVE FALLEN, EVEN WHILE LONGING TO BE FREE, AND WHO NOW LIE IN NAMELESS, UNKNOWN GRAVES, THE VICTIMS OF AMERICAN SLAVERY, THIS VOLUME IS DEDICATED.

THE KIDNAPPED

AND

THE RANSOMED.

BEING THE PERSONAL RECOLLECTIONS OF

PETER STILL AND HIS WIFE "VINA,"

AFTER FORTY YEARS OF SLAVERY.

BY

MRS. KATE E. R. PICKARD.

With an Introduction,
BY REV. SAMUEL J. MAY;

And an Appendix,
BY WILLIAM H. FURNESS, D.D.

THIRD EDITION.

SYRACUSE:
WILLIAM T. HAMILTON.

NEW YORK AND AUBURN:
MILLER, ORTON AND MULLIGAN.
1856.

Title page of The Kidnapped and the Ransomed

Today *The Kidnapped and the Ransomed* sits quietly on some library shelves. In its time, though, it convinced thousands of readers that slavery was evil, much as Peter's talks had done when he traveled the country raising money to purchase his family's freedom.

On April 12, 1857—Easter Sunday—Charity Still suddenly became ill. She couldn't talk, apparently having suffered a stroke. Dr. James Still wrote to his sisters and brothers that "if you want to see our mother again whilst alive you must come without delay." Peter and Vina and their children rushed to her bedside, where they were joined by Charity's other children and grandchildren. She rallied briefly, managing to tell her family that she was not afraid of death. Surrounded by her sons, daughters, and grandchildren, Charity Still died on April 23, 1857, at the age of about eighty. Born a slave around the time of the Revolutionary War, she had survived to see her husband, herself, and all of her eighteen children except her two oldest, Ann and Levin, live as free people. Charity Still, or Cidney as Peter always thought of his mother, was buried next to her husband, Levin Sr., on their New Jersey farm.

A year after his mother's death, William Still became involved in a major event that helped ignite the Civil War. In March of 1858 John Brown visited the Philadelphia home of Stephen Smith, a black businessman and abolitionist. Smith invited many people to meet Brown, but few were willing to be seen with the violent white man who had taken part in murdering five proslavery settlers in Kansas. Only three people—William Still, famed black leader Frederick Douglass, and a minister—came to Smith's home to meet with John Brown.

Brown revealed a bold plan. He would raid the United States arsenal at Harpers Ferry, Virginia (now West Virginia), pass out guns from the arsenal to slaves in Virginia and Maryland, then lead a huge rebellion that would stamp out slavery. William Still opposed John Brown's scheme. There was nothing he wanted more than to end slavery, but not at the cost of hundreds, or perhaps thousands, of lives.

In October 1859 John Brown and a band of followers captured the Harpers Ferry arsenal. The huge slave rebellion never materialized, however. The arsenal was retaken by United States soldiers. Ten of Brown's followers, including two of his sons, were killed. John Brown was found guilty of treason and sentenced to die.

Several of John Brown's raiders escaped from Harpers Ferry. Two of them—Francis Meriam and Osborne Anderson—came to William Still's house to hide. Although he faced imprisonment if caught, William Still sheltered Meriam and Anderson and then sent both men on to Canada. While Brown awaited execution, his wife and daughter also stayed in the Still home. On December 2, 1859, John Brown was hanged.

John Brown's raid and execution moved the nation closer to war. Hailing Brown as a crusader against slavery, northern abolitionists tolled bells and draped buildings in black following his death. Southern whites called Brown a madman who had spread death and destruction, and they wanted everyone who had been involved in his raid punished. William Still believed that he would be arrested for helping Brown's men escape and even began making plans to flee with his family to Canada. Fortunately, though, there wasn't sufficient evidence to charge Still in the John Brown case.

William's UGRR efforts continued without letup throughout the 1850s. He helped several thousand fugitive slaves during that decade, including hundreds of children. In some single months he assisted more than fifty escaped slaves. They poured into Philadelphia right up to the time of the Civil War. For example, in 1860 twenty-four-year-old Henry Cotton came to Still, telling an amazing story of having hidden in the woods for a year in Maryland before finding his way to Philadelphia. That same year a group that reminded William of his brother Peter's family arrived at the Anti-Slavery Society Office. Jerry and Diana Mills were both about sixty years old and had come from Maryland with their twenty-seven-year-old son and two teenaged daughters. In late 1860 Harriet Tubman made her last trip as an UGRR conductor when she led Stephen and Maria Ennets and their children (six-year-old Harriet, four-year-old Amanda, and a three-month-old infant) along with two other people into the Wilmington, Delaware, area. From there, Thomas Garrett sent them on to Philadelphia, where they arrived in December. On December 1, Garrett wrote William Still a letter about this final rescue mission of Tubman's:

WILMINGTON, 12th month, 1st day, 1860

RESPECTED FRIEND:—WILLIAM STILL:— I write to let thee know that Harriet Tubman is again in these parts. She arrived last evening from one of her trips of mercy to God's poor. . . . I shall be very uneasy about them, till I hear they are safe. There is now much more risk on the road than there has been for several months past, as we find that some poor, worthless [slave catchers] are constantly on the lookout on two roads. . . . Yet as Harriet seems to have had a special angel to guard her on her journey of mercy, I have hope.

Thy Friend,
THOMAS GARRETT

Nineteen days after Garrett wrote this letter, the southern states, fearing that President Abraham Lincoln would end slavery, began seceding from the United States. Eleven states seceded, joining together as the Confederate States of America under their own president, Jefferson Davis. On the morning of April 12, 1861, the Confederates fired on Fort Sumter, a U.S. army post in South Carolina. This was the beginning of the Civil War between the Union (North) and the Confederacy (South).

Peter Still was about sixty-one years old and in declining health when the war began. Although unable to serve as a soldier, he had fought for the Union in his own way by describing slavery in speeches and in his book, *The Kidnapped and the Ransomed*. Forty-year-old William Still was also not sent to fight but supported the Union cause as best he could. The slaves were gradually freed as Union troops conquered Confederate territory. The *freedmen*, as the former slaves were called, poured into northern cities to begin new lives. In April 1862 William Still opened an office that located housing and jobs for freedmen in Philadelphia. Still was also appointed sutler (provider of supplies) at Camp William Penn, a Union army post outside Philadelphia.

In April 1865, after four bloody years of fighting, the Union won the Civil War. The conflict had claimed more American lives—nearly a million—than any other war in history. But it ended slavery forever in the United States.

"Emancipation," an engraving celebrating the freeing of the slaves; President Abraham Lincoln, who did so much to accomplish this, is pictured at the bottom.

Across the South, millions of slaves who hadn't been able to escape—people like Levin's widow Fanny, Susanna's mother Aunt Patsey, and Spencer, the man who had been cheated out of his liberty—were freed. Over were the days when a relatively small number of slaves like Charity Still and Henry "Box" Brown would try to flee to the North—sometimes succeeding, but often suffering capture, chains, and whippings. No longer would slaves save pennies like Peter Still had done to buy their families out of bondage. And no longer was there a need for Underground Railroad workers like William Still.

Peter and William Still, Harriet Tubman and Seth Concklin, Thomas Garrett and "Box" Brown's helper Samuel Smith, Ellen and William Craft, Joseph and Isaac Friedman, and thousands of other people of goodwill had won the war against slavery.

Never were people happier about seeing their brave deeds pass into history.

CHAPTER XVI

"TO THE FRIENDS OF FREEDOM"

Around New Year's Eve of 1867—almost exactly thirteen years after he was reunited with his wife and children on free soil—Peter Still became extremely ill. He had pneumonia, a very dangerous disease, especially in those days. With Vina and his children at his bedside, Peter died at about the age of sixty-eight on January 10, 1868—nineteen years to the day since the Friedman brothers had purchased him with the intention of granting him his freedom.

Unfortunately Peter Still did not live long enough to meet his grandson and namesake, young Peter. Never having known any family but his grandmother Patsey, eleven-year-old Peter apparently chose to stay in Alabama even after the remaining slaves were freed at the end of the Civil War in 1865. Finally, in 1873, perhaps after Grandmother Patsey died, nineteen-year-old Peter moved to the North to be with relatives beyond his memory—his father's side of the family. We know this because of a letter, now housed in the Historical Society of Pennsylvania, sent by William Still to his sister Mary:

Sept. 17th, 1873

Dear Mary:

Vina is stopping with us at present for a short time. Catharine brought her down last Friday. The old lady's health has been quite poorly for a long time, but she is seeming pretty [improved] now.

Peter has very recently received his son from the South and he is a smart-looking lad nearly a man's size.

Letitia [and other relatives] all send their love to you. Also Vina.

Your affectionate Bro.
W. Still

In May of 1871 the remnants of the Pennsylvania Anti-Slavery Society requested that William Still "compile and publish his personal reminiscenses and experiences relating to the Underground Railroad." William, who had retrieved his records from Lebanon Cemetery at the close of the war, immediately began writing a book. Working every day from five in the morning until eleven at night, he produced about four finished pages per day. Within a year he had written a nearly eight-hundred-page book recounting the stories of hundreds of fugitive slaves and the UGRR conductors

Catalogue of Children of Leven still and Charity his wife

Ann still was Born January 28th 1798
Leven still was Born February 26th 1799
Peter still was Born February 22 1801
Mahalah still was Born December 30th 1803
Kitty still Bos Born January 20th 1805
Samuel still was Born February 26th 1807
Mary still was Born August 31st 1808
Hannah still was Born July 31st 1810
James still was Born April 9th 1812
Isaac still was Born January 8th 1814
Johns still was Born January 8th 1815
Charles still was Born March 1st 1817
Joseph still was Born November 24th 1819
William still was Born October 7th 1821

Burlington County N J

*After reaching freedom, Charity and Levin Still Sr. made a list of
most of their children's birthdays. They may have approximated
the birthdays of their sons Levin (written Leven) and Peter, and
their daughters Mahalah and Kitturah (written Kitty), all born in
slavery. A daughter, Ann, was born before Levin, but apparently
didn't live long.*

who had helped them. At the beginning of his book, he
wrote this dedication:

TO THE FRIENDS OF FREEDOM, TO HEROIC
FUGITIVES AND THEIR POSTERITY IN THE
UNITED STATES, THESE MEMORIALS OF
THEIR LOVE OF LIBERTY ARE INSCRIBED

By the AUTHOR

After the publication of his book, *The Underground Railroad*, in early 1872, William received many letters of praise. One he especially cherished came from his old friend and mentor at the Pennsylvania Anti-Slavery Office, Reverend James Miller McKim:

March 15, 1872.

Dear William: I received your book last evening and have since been reading it with feelings of mingled pleasure and pride; pleasure at the valuable contribution which it furnishes to anti-slavery history and literature, and pride that you are the author of it. . . .

The chief value of the book will be found in its narratives, which illustrate the character of slavery, the spirit of the men engaged for its overthrow, and the difficulties which had to be overcome by these men in the accomplishment of their purpose.

A book so unique in kind, so startling in interest, and so trustworthy in its statements, cannot fail to command a large reading now and in the generations to come. That you, my long-time friend and associate, are the author of this book is to me a matter of great pride and delight. . . .

Yours ever faithfully,
J. M. McKIM

William put his niece Catharine and other relatives and friends to work selling *The Underground Railroad*. The book sold very well—thirty-five thousand copies in William's lifetime, and thousands of additional copies since then in reprint editions. Many people have tracked down relatives and family friends by studying the narratives in *The Underground Railroad*. Even today people use the book to search for lost branches of their families.

Although his book earned William Still a large income, over the years he also bought and sold real estate and operated stove, coal, and lumber businesses with great success. He became one of the wealthiest black Philadelphians of his time. Letitia and William had four children, all of whom had notable careers following college. Their oldest daughter, Caroline, was one of the first black Philadelphians to earn a medical degree and one of the first female physicians in the state of Pennsylvania. William and Letitia's daughter Frances became one of Philadelphia's first kindergarten teachers. Their son William W. worked as a public accountant and lawyer. And their son Robert was a journalist and the owner of a Philadelphia print shop.

William continued to live in Philadelphia into his old age. When the new century began, he was eighty years old and had lived to witness not only the end of slavery but the beginning of the modern civil rights movement. On July 14, 1902, William Still died of a heart attack at his Philadelphia home at the age of nearly eighty-one. At his side was Letitia Still, to whom he had been married for fifty-five years, along with their children and grandchildren. The next day's *New York Times* hailed him as the "Father of the Underground Railroad," a man who had helped thousands of people gain their freedom.

But the story of the Still family has not ended.

In 1870 Dr. James Still decided to gather his brothers and sisters for a reunion at his home in Medford, New Jersey. Peter had died two years earlier, and John Nelson Still apparently had also passed away by this time, but all of the surviving Still sisters and brothers attended. James described that first family reunion in his book, *Early Recollections and Life of Dr. James Still*:

> As this was the first gathering of the kind that occurred amongst us, a seriousness seemed to pervade the little assembly. We talked over the past and looked on each others' cheeks, all furrowed over with age. We spoke of the future, and all professed to have a hope of meeting each other in a better land. We could only congratulate each other on our present good health in our old age, and to think that seven of us brothers and sisters, out of eighteen, were now blessed to meet together.
>
> It was indeed a day of enjoyment to all. Each one had some little anecdote to relate about the past, calling to recollection some little incident that had long faded from the memory of the rest, even so far back perhaps as half a century. We talked of father and mother, and

Dr. James Still's home in Medford, New Jersey, where the first Still family reunion was held in 1870

their many hard struggles both in and out of slavery. . . . We also talked of the emancipation of the slaves in the United States by Abraham Lincoln. *Is it possible*, said we, *that we are living in a land where slavery has ceased to exist?* In this we all rejoiced greatly. We asked each other the question, *Did you expect to live to see this day?* . . .

The day of our meeting was gliding along and the Sun advancing to the western horizon, admonishing us to prepare to bid each other adieu and repair to our several homes with all the good cheer we could command. We clasped each others' hands with tears in our eyes, and bade adieu, supposing it to be the last meeting of the kind that we should enjoy this side of eternity.

But this was only their first, rather than their last, such celebration. The Still family reunion became a yearly tradition. Each summer since 1870 a member of the family has hosted a gathering of the descendants of Levin and Charity Still. The get-together has grown so huge that in 1999, at the 130th annual Still family reunion, approximately six hundred people attended.

Family members from all over the country gather for the reunion, which features a picnic and visits to sites in the Philadelphia and New Jersey areas where their ancestors lived. Skits dramatizing the deeds of Charity, Peter, William, and other ancestors are also presented. As the years pass, new generations of Still children look on, perhaps thinking of how they, too, will make the world a better place.

BIBLIOGRAPHY

Bentley, Judith. *"Dear Friend": Thomas Garrett and William Still, Collaborators on the Underground Railroad.* New York: Cobblehill Books/Dutton, 1997.

Blockson, Charles L., project director. *Philadelphia's Guide: African-American State Historical Markers.* Philadelphia: The Charles L. Blockson Afro-American Collection/ The William Penn Foundation, 1992.

McPhee, John. *The Pine Barrens.* New York: Farrar, Straus & Giroux, 1981.

Moonsammy, Rita Zorn, David Steven Cohen, and Lorraine E. Williams, editors. *Pinelands Folklife.* New Brunswick, New Jersey: Rutgers University Press, 1987.

Nash, Gary B. *Forging Freedom: The Formation of Philadelphia's Black Community, 1720–1840.* Cambridge, Massachusetts: Harvard University Press, 1988.

Pickard, Kate. *The Kidnapped and the Ransomed, Being the Personal Recollections of Peter Still and His Wife "Vina," After Forty Years of Slavery.* Philadelphia: The Jewish Publication Society of America, 1970 (reprint of 1856 edition).

Quarles, Benjamin. *Black Abolitionists.* New York: Oxford University Press, 1969.

Ripley, C. Peter, editor. *The Black Abolitionist Papers*, Volume 4. Chapel Hill: University of North Carolina Press, 1991.

Still, James. *Early Recollections and Life of Dr. James Still.* New Brunswick, New Jersey: Rutgers University Press, 1973 (reprint of 1877 edition).

Still, William. *The Underground Railroad.* New York: Arno Press and *New York Times*, 1968 (reprint of 1872 edition).

Weigley, Russell F., editor. *Philadelphia: A 300-Year History.* New York: Norton, 1982.

Also of great help were the Peter Still papers at Rutgers University in New Brunswick, New Jersey, and the William Still papers at the Historical Society of Pennsylvania in Philadelphia.

INDEX